Weapons of Mass Destruction and International Order

William Walker

ADELPHI PAPER 370

95 32456

Oxford University Press, Great Clarendon Street, Oxford OX2 6DP
Oxford New York

Athens Auckland Bangkok Bombay Calcutta Cape Town
Dar es Salaam Delhi Florence Hong Kong Istanbul Karachi
Kuala Lumpur Madras Madrid Melbourne Mexico City Nairobi
Paris Taipei Tokyo Toronto
and associated companies in Ibadan

Oxford is a trade mark of Oxford University Press

Published in the United States
by Oxford University Press Inc., New York

First published November 2004 by **Oxford University Press** for
The International Institute for Strategic Studies
Arundel House, 13–15 Arundel Street, Temple Place, London WC2R 3DX
www.iiss.org

Director John Chipman
Editor Tim Huxley
Copy Editor David Ucko
Production Simon Nevitt

British Library Cataloguing in Publication Data
Data available

Library of Congress Cataloguing in Publication Data

ISBN 0-19-856841-x
ISSN 0567-932x

Contents

Glossary

ABM	Anti-Ballistic Missile
ASEAN	Association of South-east Asian Nations
BJP	Bharatiya Janata Party
BTWC	Biological and Toxin Weapons Convention
BWC	Biological Weapons Convention
CBW	Chemical and Biological Weapons
CFE	Conventional Armed Forces in Europe Treaties
CTBT	Comprehensive Nuclear Test-Ban Treaty
CWC	Chemical Weapons Convention
FMCT	Fissile Material Cut-off Treaty
IAEA	International Atomic Energy Agency
INF	Intermediate-Range Nuclear Forces
NPT	Nuclear Non-Proliferation Treaty
NSG	Nuclear Suppliers Group
NNWS	Non-Nuclear-Weapon State
NWS	Nuclear-Weapon State
OPCW	Organisation for the Prohibition of Chemical Weapons
RMA	Revolution in Military Affairs
SDI	Strategic Defense Initiative
START I and II	Strategic Arms Reduction Treaty I and II
UN	United Nations
UNMOVIC	UN Monitoring, Verification and Inspection Commission
UNSC	UN Security Council
UNSCOM	UN Special Committee Mission
WTO	World Trade Organisation
WMD	Weapons of Mass Destruction

Introduction

The modern preoccupation with international order grew, in substantial part, out of the experiences of war in the twentieth century. Left to its own devices, the state system was obviously incapable of providing protection against technological developments which gave aggressive actors so many possibilities in warfare. On the contrary, the state system appeared to foster mass violence through its inherently competitive nature and the state's unique rights and abilities to mobilise technology for lethal purposes.

With the arrival of nuclear weapons, the preoccupation with international order assumed the quality of obsession. There *had* to be order for everyone's survival. Ironically, through its very destructiveness, the nuclear weapon itself became a primary agent of survival by discouraging war during the East–West conflict. At the same time, nuclear technology was linked to economic progress through its potential for supplying energy in large quantity. Despite these benefits, it was immediately understood that nuclear weapons and associated technologies could not be let loose within the international system. Their diffusion needed to be constrained and their application controlled. How to practise that constraint and exercise that control – effectively, legitimately and persuasively – was a challenge that had to be faced.

The nuclear order constructed during the Cold War was always precarious and controversial. Nevertheless, an approach to order was established that carried wide support and enabled the carefully managed use of nuclear weapons for deterrence purposes to coexist with the determined pursuit of non-proliferation. With the end of the Cold War, the diplomacy that underlay this approach appeared capable of fostering greater protection against weapons of mass destruction (WMD) – now including chemical and biological weapons (CBW) – and indeed of dispatching them into the margins of international relations. But this trend turned out to be deceptive. After several years of apparent progress involving substantial arms reductions and extensions to the treaty-bound framework of restraint, order turned to disorder and a common direction into a common disorientation.

In the past few years, this international order has come to resemble a metaphorical Humpty Dumpty which has suffered a great fall and is unable to return to its perch.[1] Events and trends that contributed to this fall can be readily identified: the Indian and Pakistani test explosions; the international disputes over missile defence and the Anti-Ballistic Missile (ABM) Treaty; the US turn against multilateralism; the breakdown of the United Nations Special Committee Mission (UNSCOM) in Iraq; the emergence of a more deadly terrorism exemplified by the 9/11 attacks; the subsequent 'wars on terrorism' and military actions in Iraq; and the unearthing of covert transnational supply networks. These developments all occurred against a backdrop of dramatic changes in power structure after the Soviet Union's demise and of equally dramatic changes in US political and security strategies.

This descent into disorder needs to be arrested if more devastating wars and a crippling loss of ability to solve international problems, including grave environmental problems, are to be avoided. Although the recovery of order obviously encompasses much more than WMD, recent history indicates that to qualify as such, an international order must address the dangers arising from these technologies. A re-establishment of order cannot however be achieved merely by identifying disturbing events and trends and designing policies to alleviate them, important though that task may be. It has to be rooted in an understanding of international order – and of the 'WMD order' in our context – and its historical construction and recent destabilisation. Above all, it requires an understanding of the nature and effectiveness of ordering strategies and of the forces shaping them in given periods.

This Paper is a contribution to such an understanding. It is not easily arrived at. Notions of international order and the strategies best suited to its achievement will always be contested. Furthermore, the 'problem of WMD order' is not self-contained. It is exacerbating and being exacerbated by the troubles afflicting the wider international order and the practice of international ordering, especially in the circumstances surrounding the Iraq war. Attitudes towards order also depend heavily on the position and predisposition of the observer. Inevitably, the United States requires special attention in these pages given its political and military prominence, the special responsibility it has taken upon itself since the dawn of the nuclear age, and its controversial behaviour since attaining clear hegemonic status in the 1990s.

The Paper has six chapters. The first lays out the conceptual stall and presents a distillation of the main argument, drawing especially on ideas of order and of enmity developed by Alexander Wendt, John Ikenberry, Carl Schmitt and Gabriella Slomp (an improbable quartet), which will be used to guide the analysis. The second chapter examines the development of ordering strategies pertaining to WMD up to 1990. There follows a discussion in the third chapter of the early post-Cold War period (culminating in the Nuclear Non-Proliferation Treaty (NPT) Extension Conference of 1995) and the increasing divergence of opinion over the most appropriate strategies for the changing security environment. The fourth chapter is concerned with the breakdown of order in the late 1990s and early 2000s, which occurred in two stages with the dividing line marked by the arrival of the George W. Bush administration and the attack on the Twin Towers, both occurring in 2001. The fifth chapter takes us past the Iraq War of 2003 and – with the approaching NPT Review Conference in 2005 in mind – discusses the urgent need for reinvestment in efficacy *and* legitimacy if a graver descent into disorder is to be avoided. The concluding chapter brings the discussion back to great-power relations, now including China and India, which are neglected at everyone's peril.

Chapter 1

Concepts of international order: the antidote to enmity

That a concern over order has lain at the heart of international politics in modern times is not in doubt.[1] But what meaning should the word 'order' carry? For understandable reasons, most International-Relations theorists have shied away from a definition.[2] Instead, they agree that international order means many things, that its meaning is shaped by actors' beliefs, interests and positions, that it is formed through an historically contingent combination of factors (structural, normative and instrumental), and that the presence of order is manifested by an ability to solve problems and manage change without upheaval.

The definitional difficulties are compounded by the need – usually disregarded – to distinguish between the general concept of order, alluded to when we say 'there is order', the genus of order referred to when we speak of the international order, and the various species of international order formed in particular domains or to address particular problems (regional, economic, security or otherwise). Where WMD are concerned, relations between these levels of order need to be drawn with special care. Although 'the nuclear order' is clearly *an* international order, it is intertwined with *the* international order, just as order at either level is informed by perceptions of *general* order. The awkwardness of referring to 'the WMD order' points to another difficulty, as the internal coherence of 'the nuclear order' cannot be matched when the objects of ordering differ so markedly in technology and effect. As will become evident, the gathering of a disparate set of technologies under the heading 'WMD' and their treatment under this single category contributed significantly to the difficulties encountered in the 1990s and early 2000s.

Rather than try to define order, it is most useful to focus attention on *the problem of order*, which, in the twentieth century in particular, may be seen as deriving from three linked problems of international life – those of enmity, power and legitimacy. Of the three, the problem of enmity may be considered the most fundamental – especially in a time of widespread strife such as our own – since it lies at the root of violence and war. True international order is first and foremost the antithesis of and antidote to enmity, with emphasis on the latter. The roots of enmity will not concern us here. Suffice to say that it is commonly driven by some combination of fear, ambition, grievance and, in its most intransigent form, ideological or religious disdain. Enlivened by modernity, it is this last driver of enmity that has proved so dangerous over the past century and continues to threaten even today.

Enmity's reduction to rivalry, forbearance and amity

Enmity implies enemies. Alexander Wendt writes that 'enemies lie at one end of a spectrum of role relationships governing the use of violence between Self and Other, distinct in kind from rivals and friends'.[3] Enmity exists when the Other chooses not to respect the Self's right to survival as a free subject, 'will not willingly limit its violence toward the Self', and 'therefore seeks to 'revise' the latter's life and liberty'.[4] Wendt goes on to contrast the 'deep revisionism' of enmity, where the Self and the Other can become caught up in a violent commitment to change, and the 'shallow revisionism' of rivalry, where rights to life and liberty are recognised and the Self and Other seek to revise behaviour without necessary recourse to violence.[5]

From this perspective, a primary objective of international ordering is to reduce enmity to a more benign and contained rivalry. More ambitiously, its purpose lies in reducing both enmity and rivalry to a sustained condition of forbearance or amity wherein states and other actors define their relations as intrinsically cooperative and strive to revise life and liberty by peaceful means alone. This journey from enmity towards amity, a striking feature of twentieth-century Europe, is illustrated in its idealised form in Figure 1. The objective of ordering is both to instigate movement down the figure from enmity towards forbearance and amity, and to lock states and other actors into those relations through a variety of political, economic and legal stratagems.[6] The modern conception of order and its purpose lose conviction if the movement away from enmity is easily reversed. They rely on the construction of and commitment to irreversibility.

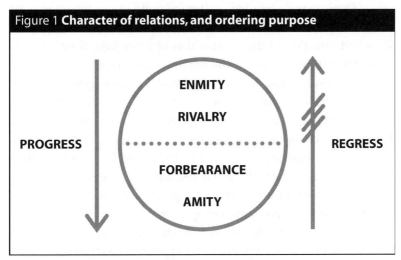

Figure 1 **Character of relations, and ordering purpose**

PROGRESS

ENMITY

RIVALRY

FORBEARANCE

AMITY

REGRESS

Since the eighteenth century, the balance of power has been the primary device for containing enmity and preventing its escalation into war. Unfortunately, there is evidence aplenty that power balancing is in itself unreliable, particularly if states are not equally committed to its sustenance, poorly led, or have unequal scope for developing their military and economic capabilities. Experience also shows that too exclusive a focus on power balancing heightens sensitivities to imbalance, which may in turn drive states into arms races and war. John Herz's security dilemma can then, through the intrinsic instability of rivalry in a dynamic political and technological environment, become a significant structural driver of enmity among states.[7] Compounding the matter, technological advance in the twentieth century and the concomitant embrace of concepts of total war dramatically increased the costs of misjudgement and breakdown in inter-state relations.

In the second half of the century, the nuclear weapon became *the* great power balancer, and the primary instrument of choice for reducing enmity between East and West to a survivable rivalry. At the same time, the thousands of nuclear weapons deployed in the name of power balancing exposed everyone and everything to deplorable risks. Similarly, moves by additional states to acquire such weapons threatened to destabilise regional power balances and to jeopardise deterrent relations among the established nuclear powers. As a consequence, 'strategic stability' and 'non-proliferation' became central preoccupations.

Over many decades, states responded to the march of technology (and especially of nuclear technology) by paying increased attention to the construction of what John Ikenberry has termed 'constitutional order' (his other two ideal types of order being 'balance of power' and 'hegemonic').[8] Without turning their backs on power balancing, they sought to overcome its deficiencies by entrenching restraint through agreements on norms, rules, institutions and practices, which would guide their behaviour. Two types of constitutionalism can be distinguished: a conservative constitutionalism through which restraint is achieved by various political and legal means, without tampering with the basic norms of the state system (sovereignty being uppermost among them); and a transformative constitutionalism through which a permanent change in behaviour is sought by fundamental institutional change. The laws of war expressed in the Hague and Geneva conventions provide examples of the first type; the League of Nations and EU are examples of the second. As we shall see, the quest for control over WMD exhibited a constitutionalism that was both conservative and transformative.

The symbiosis of power balancing and constitutionalism

Whereas Ikenberry juxtaposes the power balance and constitutional approaches to international order, the two developed symbiotically during the Cold War, at least from the Cuban missile crisis onwards. Constitutionalism helped to stabilise the balance of power, which in turn forced the superpowers to accept the restraints of constitutionalism, such as the abandonment of preventive war. It was not a case of either/or. However, constitutionalism had other purposes: to facilitate reconciliation between the contrasting rights and obligations of the nuclear 'haves' and 'have nots', provide an instrumental framework for reconciling norms of sovereignty with the intrusive verification of renunciation, and offer a means of sustaining the hope of an eventual release from the threat of nuclear extinction. In this context, constitutionalism embodied the conviction that the nuclear order was the property of all states, not just the great powers, and that they collectively possessed rights to define legitimate behaviour.[9]

Reciprocal obligation lay at the heart of the nuclear order that emerged during the Cold War and provided the essential foundation for its claim to international legitimacy. It underpinned the balance of power and permeated the international regimes, culminating in the NPT of 1968. The stark asymmetry of capabilities that the Treaty acknowledged was compensated by a highly developed symmetry of obligations among the state parties. Furthermore, the Treaty promised (the word is not too strong) that the asymmetry of capabilities would be nullified over time by the nuclear-weapon states' (NWS) practice of arms control and disarmament. Possession of nuclear arms was thus represented as a temporary trust, implying that the non-nuclear-weapon states (NNWS) were not locking themselves into permanent disadvantage through their acts of renunciation. Despite the nuclear order's political and legal distinctions between nuclear- and non-nuclear-weapon states, it thus came to resemble a classical architecture in which harmony was achieved through an acute and always rational eye toward balance and symmetry. In many ways, the nuclear order's construction assumed the ironic character of an enlightenment project.

Shifting approaches to hegemonic order

With the end of the Cold War, Ikenberry's third type of international order – hegemonic order – began to take shape. The decline of communism drained East–West relations of enmity, just as the Soviet Union's collapse removed for the time being the ability to balance US power. Instead, seen in the light of Figure 1, the political focus of the now pre-eminent power, the United States, shifted from reducing enmity through rivalry towards a more widespread realisation of forbearance and amity. Initially, constitutionalism was the United States' chosen instrument for reconstituting the highly armed political entity that had been the USSR, for addressing the emerging challenges from Iraq and North Korea, and for achieving a more extensive and irreversible commitment to the inhibition of WMD, now to include universal and verified bans on CBW. This increasingly transformative constitutionalism culminated in the NPT Extension Conference of 1995 with its universalist ambitions and collective enunciation of the 'Principles and Objectives' that would guide the next stages.

In the first years of the post-Cold War era, hegemonic order therefore developed symbiotically with constitutionalism, giving the impression of substantial continuity in ordering strategies. In the mid-1990s and for reasons both internal and external to the US, this symbiosis began to fray, gradually to be replaced by an altogether starker conception of hegemonic order. In essence, just as the WMD order reached a pinnacle of international legitimacy, it began to fail a 'test of efficacy' set mainly by influential communities within the United States. Emboldened by its new-found military supremacy, encouraged by perceived difficulties in containing the diffusion of WMD capabilities in certain regions, and radicalised by the terrorist attacks of 11 September 2001, the United States came to embrace a new approach to international order. This approach had long been advocated from the fringes, but had only briefly captured the high ground during the first Reagan administration.

The character of the new approach to order was openly displayed in the National Security Strategy published by the US government in September 2002 and in speeches and documents of the time. Its main features – the emphasis on the primacy of America's 'national interest', the freedom to express enmity (or amity) and to nominate America's friends and enemies, the downplaying of constitutionalism and multilateralism and the embrace of coercion including war – will be discussed in chapter 4. The new approach – far from the prior conception of 'legitimate international order' founded on reciprocal obligation and an enveloping mutual restraint – could not have taken firm root without 9/11, which dramatised the role of enmity in US relations with state and non-state actors and appeared to render previous approaches to international order threadbare and redundant. The terrorist attacks also provided an opportunity to draw previously hostile powers (notably Russia and China) into a circle of great powers united, however temporarily, by fear of Islamic radicalism.

What made all of this so unsettling to international order was that a kind of *double enmity* was conceived in the United States against certain actors *and* against certain conceptions of order. Underlying the understandable enmity against state and non-state actors that threatened vital interests, the US displayed a more disturbing enmity against constitutional order wherever and whenever it implied limits on American freedom of choice and action. This double enmity was highly evident in the campaign against Iraq in 2003, as enmity against the Iraqi regime was accompanied by an undisguised hostility towards United Nations (UN) processes regarding the search for WMD, the war's legitimisation and Iraq's subsequent governance and reconstruction. The resulting disturbance to international order was magnified by a pattern of behaviour evident in the defiant rejection of the Comprehensive Nuclear Test-Ban Treaty (CTBT), the Kyoto Agreement, the International Criminal Court and other constitutional initiatives with large international followings. Indeed, issues much wider than WMD were involved. As we shall see later, a perception grew outside the US that the problems of WMD were, in some measure, being 'surfed' in order to institute a new type of hegemonic order.

The United States' recasting of its hegemonic strategy was accompanied by, and promoted through, an attack on the constitutionalism that it had done so much to develop but which influential elites had long resented and distrusted. Whilst promulgated as a means of protection against WMD, the new security strategy was deeply subversive to the prevailing WMD order. To the US administration, the latter was worthless if it could not 'roll back' the weapon programmes of states that defied it. To others, the turn to coercion, and the casting aside of the norms of reciprocal obligation and mutual restraint, threatened a much wider malaise. The United States' reorientation was particularly unsettling to lesser powers given that it had hitherto respected and relied upon as the great champion of a legitimate international order founded on cooperation and shared norms.

Carl Schmitt's three realms of enmity

In so expressing its hegemonic intent and will, the United States under George W. Bush's presidency discarded the liberal and realist mantles of statesmen and scholars such as Dean Acheson and Hans Morgenthau, which had shaped its ordering strategies since 1945. In their place, the US adopted an interpretation of and approach to international order that bore considerable resemblance to those propounded by the German political theorist Carl Schmitt. In *The Concept of the Political*, published in 1932, Schmitt moved enmity into the foreground of political life, claiming that the division of social groupings into friends and enemies 'defined the political' since it stimulated the formation of identity and of political action on its behalf.[10] In his later *Theorie des Partisanen* of 1962, Schmitt went further by proposing three categories or realms of enmity, which he termed 'conventional', 'true' and 'absolute' enmity.[11]

By conventional enmity, Schmitt referred to that realm in which social units (notably states) recognise each other's rights to engage in relations of friendship or enmity and devise various individual and collective stratagems to ensure survival. They bind themselves in and through convention. From long-term interaction stems a certain regularity in the relations among competing states, which finds one of its expressions (doomed to frustration, in Schmitt's view) in the attempts to limit or abolish war.

True enmity, in contrast, is the enmity felt by the partisan, guerrilla or terrorist group towards a powerful actor that it perceives as unjustifiably dominating a people's territory or society and violating its identity. Such enmity is indelibly marked by asymmetry, irregularity and the absence of mercy. It is asymmetrical because the dominating power has far greater resources at its disposal. It is irregular because the opposing groups can only inflict significant injury by disregarding conventions governing the use of force, and because popular support for a cause can be expanded if the dominating power can itself be enticed into irregularity. Finally, it is an enmity marked by an absence of mercy as either side is bent on the destruction of the Other, allowing no quarter.

According to Schmitt, absolute enmity is true enmity taken to extremes by the opposing group's revolutionary or millenarian intent.[12] The enmity of the partisan, guerrilla or political terrorist is potentially satiable or reducible if the opposing power departs or offers satisfying concessions. Group tactics are oriented towards winning these concessions and are usually tailored to avoid unduly antagonising host populations. Absolute enmity is however insatiable and its bearers are more likely to adopt extreme violence in pursuit of their revolutionary aims. Once absolute enmity is galvanised, there can be no substantial concessions as they would be too dangerous to the state and the state's confidence in itself. Al-Qaeda currently typifies this absolute enmity, an enmity that is made more attractive to disaffected communities by its claim to have political as well as ideological objectives (the combining of true and absolute enmity is arguably the most potent force of all).

If one accepts Schmitt's typology, which seems convincing, it follows that architects of international order now have to contend, more than ever before in modern times, with enmity in two dimensions. In one dimension lies the enmity between states within the state system and its 'reduction', through various ordering strategies, to rivalry, forbearance or amity. In the other dimension lies enmity between states and insurgent groups, the latter now operating with greater technological resources and in globalised and media-soaked environments that are rich in opportunities. In this second dimension, the 'reduction' of enmity needs to be addressed through a different if not wholly different repertoire of measures (counter-terrorism, peace processes etc.). The catch, however, is that if the Other's enmity towards the Self is deemed to be absolute, and if the Other is able to create mass anxiety and injury through recourse to weapons of mass destruction or mass effect, the threatened state may be drawn in its desperation to avoid devastating surprise attacks into a strategy of pure elimination and into curtailment of freedoms of movement and association. This is essentially what has happened internationally since 9/11.

Here, three points merit particular attention. First, such absolute transnational threats can, if real or portrayed as real, powerfully affect confidence in the state's ability to protect its people, and in the state's ability to generalise that protection. They are therefore potent agents of progressive or reactionary change in security norms and practices. Second, managing the interface between the two dimensions, both to discourage cooperation between states and insurgent groups and to harmonise norms and security practices across boundaries, becomes a difficult but necessary activity in international politics. The recent story of Iraq has shown the perils of mismanaging this task. Third and despite all of the above, the achievement of order in the first and inter-state dimension has to retain primacy. States possess by far the greatest capacity to perpetrate violence, and remain the primary holders of authority and creators of order – and disorder – on the international stage. Without durable and cooperative relations among states, and especially among great powers, there can be no solution to the problem of enmity in either dimension.

'Politics is created to make real enmity impossible'

Just as the security environment has become more complex and perilous, sharp divisions have emerged over the strategies that states should adopt singly and in cooperation with one another. Although disagreements on specific policy measures are to be expected, there is worry that the divisions run deeper – that they are rooted in increasingly irreconcilable views of the nature and purpose of politics, especially as regards the role of enmity and the possibility of its restraint. There is concern that politics generally, and US politics in particular, are taking a Schmittean turn away from the broad consensus that has informed political thought and action over the past several decades. Gabriella Slomp recently observed that, for Schmitt, 'politics can never abolish enmity as the latter is the very essence of politics ... politics as a struggle of friends and enemies is in our history as well as our destiny'.[13] For Schmitt, humankind is trapped in this struggle, indeed resistance to it is culturally demeaning as it deprives societies of their identities and thus of existential meanings. She contrasts Schmitt's views with those of Thomas Hobbes and most subsequent political theorists and practitioners, whether of conservative or liberal hues.[14] For Hobbes, 'politics is created to make real enmity impossible', or is created at least to facilitate the escape from enmity.[15] Identity is not and should not be formed primarily by dividing groups into friends and enemies. Indeed, modern societies can neither tolerate nor survive the habitual violence implied by such unchecked divisions.

From this perspective, the character of American political strategy under the Bush administration is not essentially Schmittean. A strong current of belief in the peace-creating influence of US culture and political doctrine remains. This being the case, there should be no fundamental transatlantic disagreement over the 'concept of the political' nor over the purpose of international order. Politics and order are created to make enmity impossible, notwithstanding the fact that they can also foment enmity if pursued imperiously. The main argument is over means rather than ends. The claim is that, although generally well intentioned, the political strategies being advocated by either side are making enmity possible rather than impossible. Advocates (stereotypically in Europe) of an extended constitutionalism stand accused of ignoring or being soft on transgressors, thereby undermining the very constitutionalism that they champion. Advocates (stereotypically in the US) of a more confrontational approach to transgressors, often entailing the use of force, stand accused of fomenting enmity and of disturbing the 'regularities' of international relations as expressed through international laws and norms and through the practice of diplomacy.

Although the disagreement has run deep, these observations suggest that there is after all a common ground. It entails movement, from one side towards a more muscular practice of constitutionalism, and from the other side towards an exercise of hegemonic power that is accompanied by a revitalisation of that same constitutionalism. However, that common ground cannot be reached just by deciding how to respond to individual problems, threats or actors (such as Iran today). It requires an engagement of minds at the level of high political strategy, an engagement that is mutual and resistant to the overbearing veto of any one state or community.

Any route into this high strategy must rest upon an understanding of what it takes to construct a robust international order, and how that task has been addressed since the arrival of WMD. In seeking this understanding, no apology is needed for returning to the past, even to the now quite distant past when nuclear weapons first emerged onto the international stage. Any claim that 'everything changed' after 9/11 or with the end of the Cold War deserves to be rejected out of hand. There is (and has to be) continuity as well as discontinuity – continuity of situation, of problem and solution, and of commitment. Distinguishing what has and has not changed and must and must not change is the difficult task facing any responsible government. Before considering the present day, it is therefore necessary to return to history, not to recount it as such but to identify features relevant to our understandings of international order and its achievement.

Chapter 2

Weapons of Mass Destruction and International Order to 1990

The nuclear weapon's arrival and the early struggle for order

From the middle of the nineteenth century, the increasingly organised development and diffusion of technology both complicated and fuelled the quest for international order. States sought three kinds of solutions outside war. One was to regulate technological activity and set limits on military outputs and deployments. Examples include the naval-arms control agreements of the late nineteenth century and the disarmament agreements incorporated in the Versailles Treaty of 1919. A second approach entailed more extensive laws of war, notably through the Hague and Geneva Conventions, in order to place limits on the conditions under and manner in which wars would be waged. The third approach involved a shift from a competitive to an intrinsically cooperative international order and the legal binding of states into cooperation and the collective punishment of transgressors. This was the League of Nation's quest for a perpetual amity.

In 1925, 41 states signed the Geneva Protocol, banning the use in war of chemical and bacteriological weapons. Although a weak treaty by modern standards, this was the first time that the exploitation of a field of technology for military purposes had been prohibited. The ban was sought out of humanitarian concern over the terrible injuries caused by chemical weapons to combatants and non-combatants alike, and out of the military calculation that chemical weapons had impeded rather than aided advances in warfare.[1]

The chemical weapon was recognised as being different – offensive to culture and deserving to be singled out for prohibition among the plethora of new weapons becoming available to states. However it was not viewed as a weapon threatening mass destruction, a notion born in the experiences of Hiroshima and Nagasaki. The first approximate use of the term 'weapon of mass destruction' occurred in January 1946 when the UN General Assembly, in its very first resolution, established 'a Commission to Deal with the Problems Raised by the Discovery of Atomic Energy'.[2] The Commission was instructed to make specific proposals 'for the elimination from national armaments of atomic weapons and of all other major weapons adaptable to mass destruction'.[3] The precise wording 'weapon of mass destruction' was then adopted in August 1948 when the UN Commission for Conventional Armaments had to decide which weapons to exclude from its remit.[4] The term was thus chosen out of bureaucratic convenience to denote that set of weapons that would not be called conventional. Stigmatisation rather than any common military or technological property caused them to be grouped together.

The term 'weapon of mass destruction' soon fell out of common usage. It was dropped mainly because the nuclear weapon rapidly attained a political and strategic significance that towered above that of the other weapons. A hierarchy of stigmatised weapons established itself with nuclear weapons maintaining a clear primacy ahead of chemical and then biological weapons. The 'weapons of mass destruction' were only reconnected in the 1990s following the end of the Cold War, leading to today's habitual political reference to 'WMD' as a single undifferentiated category.

Why did the nuclear weapon attract such attention? Here was a weapon with the capacity to destroy entire states, peoples, cultures and ecologies. Its existence implied a form of absolute enmity (as Schmitt emphasised in *Theorie des Partisanen*), a willingness to contemplate the total destruction of the Other or even all Others. It thus created an inescapable practical and moral obligation to avoid this fate, an obligation falling especially upon the shoulders of any state possessing the capability.

At the same time, the bombing of Hiroshima and Nagasaki had demonstrated the weapon's enormous political and military utility. Although its role in ending the war with Japan is still debated, it was widely perceived to have hastened Japan's surrender and averted a larger loss of life.[5] Particularly in the United States, the atomic bomb came to be regarded as a just means of ending a just war. The potential for nuclear weapons to acquire routine legitimacy in the eyes of their holders was thereby established. Furthermore, it quickly became evident that the nuclear weapon conferred power and prestige on its possessor, and that pride in ownership could drive the abhorrence of their effects out of the public mind.

The invention of the nuclear weapon thus gave rise to three powerful but contradictory pressures in international politics. The first was to eliminate the weapon and thereby remove the threat of extinction along with the temptation to acquire such an extreme form of coercion. However as the East–West conflict took root in 1945 and 1946, cooperation on elimination quickly became unrealisable, rendering such a difficult task impossible.[6] The second pressure was for states to acquire the weapon so as to expand national power and prestige and to balance or gain ascendancy over adversaries. The third combined the first and second: to arm the Self whilst preventing the armament of Others.

Although the initial priority was to constrain the diffusion of knowledge, anxiety over the aggressive future use of nuclear weapons led the United States and later the Soviet Union to debate the use of preventive war as the ultimate route to safety. As the US could not hope to defeat the Soviet Union by conventional means, a war to eliminate the emerging Soviet nuclear capability had to be a nuclear war.[7] Preventive war was thus only conceivable in these circumstances so long as the US maintained its nuclear dominance. Similar debates occurred in the USSR in the 1960s, but with China as the planned target. In the event, the US and later the USSR calculated that the costs, including those of prestige, would be too severe to justify recourse to nuclear preventive war. Although the avoidance of surprise attacks continued to preoccupy either side throughout the Cold War, it was always framed by the deterrent relationship and the knowledge that neither state would avoid extensive damage in nuclear war.

With the arrival of the hydrogen bomb in 1953, preventive war against a proliferating state was expunged from the American policy lexicon, not to return for almost half a century. Notwithstanding the recurrent debates about limited nuclear war, states – particularly those that risked nuclear retaliation – subscribed in large part to Bernard Brodie's observation in 1946: 'thus far the chief purpose of our military establishment has been to win wars. From now on its chief purpose must be to avert them'.[8] Thenceforth, the formation of a nuclear order was animated by a desire to prevent enmity among the major powers from spilling over into catastrophic war. Deterrence became king. The downside was that the restraint of enmity through deterrence required a constant preparation for war, and a constant commitment to engage in catastrophic war if the nuclear-armed adversary stepped out of line.

This was the reality of the East–West balance of terror established in the mid- to late 1950s. By that time, three thresholds had been crossed: into nuclearisation after the early test explosions and deployments; from the atomic bomb to the more powerful thermonuclear weapon; and then into a technology-saturated deterrent relationship involving arms racing and the mass production of warheads and missiles. The opportunity to hold the US and USSR to a 'minimum deterrent' involving a few hundred rather than tens of thousands of weapons on either side was missed. This was a substantial failure, complicating if rendering still more essential the subsequent achievement of arms control.

There remained the problem of nuclear proliferation and an awkward question that would later be posed most persuasively by Kenneth Waltz: if nuclear weapons compelled the US and USSR and for that matter the UK, France and China to behave with restraint, why should their gradual diffusion not be allowed to usher in a more general restraint and avoidance of war?[9] Why should states' rights to use nuclear deterrence be restricted rights? The adopted answers held that the risks of nuclear war would rise with the number of nuclear-armed states, and that weapon programmes would incite regional enmities and arms racing. Furthermore, states with histories of military aggression and fanaticism were not to be allowed access to a technology that could be used to launch fresh bids for power and position (Germany and Japan then being the pertinent cases). By the early 1960s, the elevation of non-proliferation from a specific goal to an international norm had acquired momentum as a pragmatic response to the threatening spread of nuclear weaponry. The task of instituting a non-proliferation regime was taken up in earnest once the USSR realised the dangers that it would face from an uncontrolled diffusion of nuclear weapons, many of which could end up being targeted against it.

To complicate matters, the desire to inhibit the spread of nuclear technology had to be reconciled with the powerful urge to allow the science and technology of nuclear energy to diffuse so that its economic benefits could be widely enjoyed. States and firms of all kinds claimed their fundamental rights of inclusion in the civilian technological enterprise, especially during decolonisation when new states sought to emulate industrialisation and escape poverty. Although civil nuclear trade would not take off until the 1960s, an expectation of participation had already taken root by the time of President Dwight Eisenhower's announcement of Atoms for Peace in 1953.

The emergent Cold War nuclear order: managed deterrence and abstinence

For all its horrors, the great discovery of the Cold War was that an effective and legitimate international order could, given persistence and good judgement, be constructed to handle the dangers and contradictions of the nuclear age. This order began to acquire a coherent and legitimate institutional form in the 1960s. In an article published a few years ago, the author suggested that the emerging order comprised two linked systems of cooperative endeavour – a managed system of deterrence, and a managed system of abstinence.[10] Although the word 'system' is problematic in this context, it has some justification given the high interconnectedness evident in each field and the deeply technological nature (technological here used in its broadest sense) of the solutions provided.[11] The two systems may be described thus:

- a managed system of deterrence, whereby a recognised set of states continued (for the time being) to use nuclear weapons to curb enmity and maintain stability, but in a manner that was increasingly controlled and rule-bound;
- a managed system of abstinence, whereby other states abandoned their sovereign rights to develop, hold and use such weapons whilst retaining rights to develop nuclear energy for civil purposes in return for economic, security and other benefits.

The system of deterrence involved, among other things:

- nuclear hardware deployed by the nuclear powers with extensive command-and-control systems and hotlines installed to aid communication in sudden crises;
- sets of understandings and practices, expressed in the deterrence theories of Brodie, Schelling and others and enunciated in nuclear doctrine, of how nuclear and conventional forces should be deployed and managed to ensure mutual vulnerability and restraint;[12]
- the establishment of bilateral arms control processes, engaging policy elites in dialogue and limiting missile deployments and anti-missile defences through binding treaties.

The system of abstinence involved, for its part:

- the nuclear umbrellas (extended deterrence) held over allies of the US and USSR, and incorporated in NATO, the Warsaw Pact and the US–Japan Security Treaty, which made allied NNWS feel reasonably secure despite their lack of nuclear weapons;
- the non-proliferation regime founded and developed especially through the NPT of 1968, which rested inter alia upon the reciprocal obligations of two classes of state, the NWS (limited legally to the five states that had undertaken test explosives before 1967) and the NNWS;[13]
- an instrumental machinery to verify (through international safeguards) states' renunciations through rigorous accounting and inspection of the materials and technologies used for civil purposes, and to prevent (through export controls) weapon-related materiel from being transferred across boundaries without proper consent and regulation.[14]

The order described here was always precarious and dangerous. It was also twice thrown off balance soon after its establishment. First, the 1973–74 energy crisis and the Indian test explosion of 1974 aroused fears of an unstoppable spread of weapon capabilities as states invested in plutonium fuel-cycles. The US government under Presidents Ford and Carter responded by pressing for stringent constraints on the development of and trade in fuel-cycle technologies, a move that was widely criticised.[15] The second occasion related to President Reagan's launch in the early 1980s of the Strategic Defense Initiative (SDI), or Star Wars project, in the apparent desire to regain supremacy over the USSR and safety from attack.[16] Despite causing major disturbance and leaving some debris, both crises blew over. From the early 1960s until well into 1990s, the nuclear order described above demonstrated an essential stability and effectiveness.

Two other facets of this international nuclear order deserve attention: the legitimacy attained by embedding ideas of progress and universality; and the dominant role taken by the United States in its development.

Legitimacy, progress and universality

A nuclear order that so blatantly institutionalised the division between nuclear armed and unarmed states, and that allowed some but not other states to use nuclear weapons as 'antidotes to enmity', would inevitably struggle to achieve international legitimacy, not least because the UN Charter recognised the equal sovereign rights of states to self-defence. Yet the nuclear order had to achieve wide international legitimacy if states were to opt into it and remain committed over the long term. In the event, legitimacy was built upon several foundations. These included the adoption of the non-proliferation norm; the sharing of civil technology; the nuclear powers' tacit commitment not to resort to preventive war and their increasingly formal commitment (through 'negative security assurances') not to use nuclear weapons against NNWS. The legitimising process was further abetted by the development of a safeguard system that was intrusive yet respected the norms of state sovereignty, and the commitment of the NPT's NWS parties to uphold both the systems of deterrence and abstinence in a manner that served the common good.

Above all, the problem of legitimacy was addressed by embedding a progressive ideal in the NPT, resting upon the assumption that a world rid of nuclear weapons would be more orderly, just and resilient to catastrophe and the manipulation of great powers. Complete nuclear disarmament was therefore the goal towards which all states should strive, irrespective of the international system's anarchic nature. The legitimacy of the NPT's arrangements thus rested heavily on the notion that possession of nuclear weapons by the acknowledged powers – the US, USSR and UK in the first instance – was a temporary trust, and that the Cold War's expansion of armament should eventually be followed by an irreversible contraction. Given this progressive ambition, non-proliferation could gain political and moral primacy over proliferation, and actions leading to weapons proliferation – the right to self-defence notwithstanding – could be invested with illegitimacy.

This progressive ideal had political utility. The US and the USSR were able to draw members of their alliance systems into the non-proliferation regime through hegemonic persuasion. However, non-aligned and neutral states had to be convinced that the non-proliferation regime was other than a neo-colonial device for reasserting hierarchy, that the commitment to control nuclear arms was genuine, and that the regime would bring them economic and security advantages.

The progressive ideal went hand-in-hand with notions of universalism. The NPT explicitly proclaimed the abhorrence of nuclear war in any form, and the universal validity of non-proliferation and disarmament policies. Universalism permeated the nuclear order in another important respect: it implied the assumption (or necessary faith) that all states would behave alike in the face of massive danger, and that their behaviour would conform to a predictable rationality. Nuclear deterrence could therefore be relied upon, as could states' general predilection towards honouring international undertakings. Trust and rationality, trust in rationality: they went hand in hand.

All in all, the nuclear order's legitimacy developed around an acknowledgement of reciprocal obligation, a commitment to cooperate in the social and political interest, and a shared trust in rational process.

The United States' assumption of special responsibility

From the outset, the United States struck up an exceptional relationship with nuclear weapons. It is an historical fact that the nuclear weapon's origins lay in Europe: it was the product of the scientific discoveries of the late nineteenth and early twentieth centuries to which the United States contributed little. The knowledge spread to the US as a result of political turmoil in Europe and the subsequent emigration of Jewish and other scientists to the United States in the 1930s and early 1940s.[17] The Manhattan Project began as a multinational exercise but ended with an American weapon. The Project was in effect nationalised by US financing, its conduct on US territory, the adoption of US citizenship by many of the European participants, and above all by the American act of using the weapon in war. What is more, it became an American weapon just as the United States was emerging from the Second World War as a global power.

This had important consequences. In a significant sense, the United States did not feel responsible for the birth of the atomic bomb, which had arisen from the malevolence of Others, not from the desires of the Self. Yet US policy elites did feel an immediate and unique responsibility for creating some kind of order in face of the many dangers and predicaments that followed the weapon's invention. Others could not be trusted or entrusted with the task. The US quest for order became bound up with the broader struggle to manage its newly acquired hegemony; with the Soviet Union's challenge, which immediately gained a strong nuclear dimension; and with the attempt to implement an international order based on the UN Charter. The international stance adopted by the United States towards nuclear weapons therefore became pastoral and monarchical, proactive and managerial, with the problems of nuclear and international order intertwining from the outset. Substituting WMD for nuclear weapons, this observation remains as valid today as it did in the years after 1945.

Immediately following Hiroshima, two diametrically opposed concepts of order became apparent within the United States, each with its strong backing. One sought solutions in cooperative action and the creation of constitutional mechanisms for achieving restraint, including the United States' self-restraint to encourage international conformity with its proposals. This approach found expression in the Acheson-Lilienthal Report and Baruch Plan of 1946. The other concept of order involved the United States using its technological advantage to assert supremacy so as to guarantee its security and create international order in its image. In the event, neither approach proved tenable. The subsequent US internal and external struggle to create order entailed a contest between these two conceptions of order and a search for a means of reconciling them.

The Reagan interlude apart, the nuclear order that emerged in the Cold War succeeded in incorporating both conceptions. To borrow Ikenberry's terminology, it involved a sophisticated symbiosis of constitutional, balance of power and hegemonic strategies. Deterrence entailed the calculated balancing of power (or terror) by the superpowers; the whole order (deterrence and abstinence) was deeply constitutional insofar as it was 'organised around agreed-upon legal and political institutions that operated to allocate rights and limit the exercise of power' and held international law in the highest regard.[18] It was also hegemonic, insofar as the US and USSR were the dominant powers within their alliance systems. Both states became increasingly wedded to constitutionalism by their inescapable needs to stabilise nuclear deterrence, sustain legitimacy, and ensure compliance with international obligations.

This blend of strategies was reflected in the spread of bureaucratic responsibilities within government. In the United States in particular, no single agency came to dominate policy formation. The Departments of Defense, State and Energy and various other governmental agencies came to share (by and large and in most periods) a similar notion of international order and of the ordering strategies that the United States should pursue. This involved in particular the Department of Defense imbibing constitutionalism and the Department of State the balance of power. As we shall see later, this blended approach would be replaced in the late 1990s and early 2000s. At that point, a more singular approach emerged, led by a Department of Defense and its political and industrial allies eager to free the US from the constraining effects of constitutionalism and to exploit its superior military and technological assets.

Chapter 3

The post-Cold War WMD order: two divergent paths

What we commonly call the post-Cold War era began with three extraordinary events: the end of the Cold War itself (occurring between 1986 and 1990), the first Gulf War, and the break-up of the Soviet Union, both in 1991. Along with its recovery of technological dominance in both civil and military fields, each of these events increased the power and prestige of the United States, as did its economic rejuvenation and Japan and Germany's lapses into economic stagnation. More than ever before, the US found itself taking the lead in shaping and re-shaping international order, which also reinforced its sense of exceptional rights and responsibilities.

From the outset, two quite different views emerged in the United States on the prospect for and means of achieving international order in this changed environment. One was optimistic and cosmopolitan, the other pessimistic and nationalistic, the one placing its trust in politico-legal and the other in politico-military solutions. Initially the first dominated, but by the end of the 1990s the second had gained ascendancy. Partly because of 9/11, the first years of the twenty-first century brought a radicalisation of this second approach along with a belief that the problem of order had changed fundamentally. Pundits in Washington placed emphasis on discontinuity and on the redundancy of old orders and approaches to order. This outlook was not shared elsewhere to anything like the same extent. Rather than accept the US interpretation and the aggressive behaviour it seemed to advocate, most other governments remained committed to the prior concept of international order, which they preferred to adapt rather than abandon. The result was schism.

The purpose of this chapter is to consider the ordering approach adopted in the early post-Cold-War period and how and why it came to be supplanted in the second half of the 1990s. How did WMD feature in this transition? Why did they move towards the margins and then back towards the centre of international discourse?

Path 1: Towards the cooperative reduction and elimination of all WMD

After the dramatic events of the late 1980s and early 1990s, four questions relating to WMD had to be addressed. First, how could the armaments amassed over the Cold War be safely and expeditiously reduced? Second, how could one ensure that the disintegration and internal transformation of a nuclear superpower did not cause more problems than it solved? Third, what would be the best way of disarming Iraq and North Korea and dealing with other offenders against international laws and norms? Fourth, what would be the best response to the renewed sense of danger associated with CBW?

A first observation is that the approaches adopted in the early to mid-1990s meshed with a new formula for establishing order and eliminating enmity. The new international order would arise from the combined forces of globalisation, democratisation, the rule of law and cooperative security. Globalisation and economic liberalisation would draw states into a deeper interdependence; democratisation would spread and entrench non-violent modes of interaction; international law would bind states and peoples to commonly agreed standards of behaviour; and the great issues of the day could be addressed cooperatively through multilateral processes. The widely-shared ambition was to shift inter-state relations at global and regional levels from the top half of Figure 1 towards a permanent condition of forbearance and amity, and to bind all actors into that condition through institutional and legal processes. The success of the EU and, perhaps, of the Association of South-east Asian Nations (ASEAN) showed what was achievable in regions where enmity had previously seemed endemic.

Taking advantage of Mikhail Gorbachev's and Boris Yeltsin's efforts to normalise relations with the US and of the simultaneous drive by China under Deng Xiaoping to engage with the outside world, advocates of 'the new international order' placed their trust in a heightened constitutionalism aided by an expansion of economic interaction. The United States would use its increased hegemonic authority to lead this constitutional project and would accept some restraint of its own power in return for greater international order. Where WMD were concerned, the goal was marginalisation. The system of deterrence might remain in place, but more as an insurance against backsliding than as a foundation of any future order. The system of abstinence would instead take centre stage and would begin to draw the nuclear-armed states into its embrace. Thus the late 1980s and early 1990s brought a series of important arms-reduction agreements, including the Intermediate-Range Nuclear Forces (INF), the Strategic Arms Reduction Treaty I and II (START I and II) and the Conventional Armed Forces in Europe Treaties (CFE Treaties). Moreover, beyond these agreements lay a commitment to develop measures such as the nuclear test ban which would inhibit both weapons acquisition by additional states and the development of new weapon designs.

Managing the break-up of a nuclear superpower

Between 1991 and 1994, a transition occurred within the former Soviet space from a single monolithic state, heavily armed with nuclear weapons deployed across its territories, to twelve sovereign states of which only one – Russia – retained nuclear arms and capabilities for manufacturing them. This was an astonishing feat, achieved largely through political negotiation and with hardly a shot fired. Above all, it was achieved through a strict adherence to constitutional norms and proprieties. In particular:

- *Norms of sovereignty and sovereign rights to exist.* It was acknowledged that new states would be established within the pre-defined borders of the former Soviet republics. Despite Russia's predominant size and power, the re-founded Russian state did not challenge the rights of the new states to exist, nor did it mount irredentist challenges to the new states through the Russian minorities living within their frontiers. As such, Russia worked with its new neighbours to avoid the surfacing of old enmities that could have derailed the entire project and brought a return to violence and oppression Thus, a state system could emerge in the former Soviet political space without the units being drawn into a struggle for survival and supremacy in which nuclear weapons might have gained an immediate salience.

- *Russia's recognition as the USSR's successor state.* Russia's emergence as the successor state to the Soviet Union had three aspects: juridical (inheriting the rights and responsibilities of the USSR under international law); the retention of identity (inheriting the status of a great power); and guardianship (inheriting control over the USSR's nuclear materiel).[1] Although the Russian Federation had no legally enshrined right to assume the USSR's mantle either as permanent member of the UN Security Council (UNSC) or as NWS party to the NPT, its recognition by the US and other states in these roles was judicious. Some authority-laden entity had to take charge of the massive capabilities assembled by the Soviet Union, and it quickly became apparent that Russia's preparedness to cooperate in this and other fields was contingent upon the granting of high international status and rights to possess nuclear weapons.

- *Adherence to arms control agreements and to non-proliferation norms and rules.* The INF and START I treaties provided a legal and instrumental framework for removing and destroying weapons located in territories outside Russia. These treaties and their presumed successors also provided confidence among the new states that Russia would remain bound to arms reduction and regulation. Whilst Russia took over the USSR's membership of the NPT, all 11 states had to join the Treaty as NNWS and submit themselves to international safeguards in order to receive the international recognition and economic assistance that they craved.

- *Russia's opening of its nuclear production estate.* Faced with the enormous problems of dealing with the USSR's nuclear legacies, the Russian state displayed an unprecedented willingness to allow its sovereignty to be penetrated by outsiders (including NGOs). In return for injections of finance through the Cooperative Threat Reduction Programme, US scientists, technicians and regulators opened a dialogue with their Russian counterparts and gained access to many of Russia's nuclear sites. This collaboration was intended to avoid leakage of nuclear materiel to other states and to assist in the dismantling of redundant weapons and materials. Although many difficulties were encountered, interaction replaced the total exclusion that had been practised hitherto.[2]

The constitutionalism that had come to underpin the general international order and the specific nuclear order thus proved enormously valuable in ensuring a non-violent and reasonably stable outcome. It provided clear normative guidance, enabled states to coordinate their policies, created incentives for states to 'play by the rules', and helped to create an atmosphere – especially important for the weaker states – in which the interests of great powers could be meshed with the pursuit of universal norms. As a consequence, the USSR's collapse strengthened confidence in the utility and vitality of constitutional approaches to international politics, for the time being at least. It delivered a 'positive shock' to international order, as did the contemporaneous Gulf War in its demonstration of diverse states' willingness to use force to counter military aggression.

The multilateral disarmament of Iraq

The Gulf War nevertheless delivered a 'negative shock' to that part of the constitutional order consisting of non-proliferation regime of the constitutional order. It revealed serious shortcomings in the international safeguards system, which had been blind to activities pursued by a state determined to elude its watchful eye, and in the export-control system, which had failed to prevent Iraq from acquiring the technologies needed for WMD design and production. It thus highlighted the dangers of clandestine programmes and the failure to reveal them in good time. Above all, Iraq's behaviour challenged the society of states to respond effectively to a blatant violation of its norms and rules.

Three innovations were attempted in response. First, authority for disarming Iraq was vested in the UN, which, through its Security Council, established UNSCOM and gave it and the International Atomic Energy Agency (IAEA) the powers required to eliminate Iraq's WMD capabilities. In so doing, international inspectors were granted unconditional access to all sites on Iraqi territory. Iraq's full sovereignty would only be restored, economic sanctions removed, and the threat of war lifted when the task was completed.

Second, pushed by the United States, a wholesale reform of the nuclear safeguards system's rules and procedures was negotiated between 1993 and 1997 (the '93+2 Program' leading to the 'Additional Protocol').[3] Sensitive to state sovereignty, NPT safeguards had hitherto limited IAEA access to facilities declared by the state. Under the reformed safeguards, NNWS parties to the NPT would be required to accept a much deeper penetration of national sovereignty. Among other things, inspections could be mounted 'any time, any place', monitoring instruments could be installed outside declared facilities, states would have to provide the IAEA with design information before facilities were operated, and the Agency could in future draw upon intelligence information provided by member states.

Third, a substantial revision of the Nuclear Suppliers' Guidelines was agreed in 1993 among members of the Nuclear Suppliers Group (NSG). Drawn up in the 1970s, the Guidelines had mainly covered exports of nuclear materials and of the engineering systems required for their production. Henceforth, exporters would require national permits to trade in a wide range of dual-use goods as well as in equipment used for weapon manufacture. NSG members also agreed to strengthen export-licensing processes and to introduce tougher domestic laws and penalties for transgressors. In essence, they extended the scope of nuclear-export controls to the whole field of high technology, an ambitious task in a rapidly globalising environment. Equivalent moves were taken to strengthen export controls pertaining to CBW and to ballistic missiles.

Taken together and if sustained, these innovations seemed to move constitutionalism onto a new plane. They strengthened the authority of the UN and its agencies, and they anticipated instrumental developments involving a much greater – and still legitimate – penetration of national sovereignty and coordination of regulatory activity.

The NPT Extension Conference of 1995

At the heart of the nuclear order lay the NPT, the institution that bound states into the order and gave it normative coherence. Unusually for a security treaty, it was given a limited lifetime; in 1995, 25 years after its entry into force, member states had to decide whether it should survive and for how long. Three observations are pertinent here.[4]

First, the prospect of this event and its obvious significance encouraged policy makers in all relevant states to reassess their relations with the Treaty and its contribution to their present and future security. In the early 1990s, the US government was already signalling that it regarded the Treaty as fundamental to international order in the post-Cold-War environment and that it would press for its indefinite extension. Most other member states shared this evaluation even if many feared that the proposal for permanence would embolden the NWS to regard their possession of nuclear weapons as a permanent right. The desire to be involved in the Extension Conference also played a part in the decisions of a number of important states to join the Treaty prior to 1995. They included China and France, who in 1992 joined the US, Russia and the UK as NWS under the Treaty; and Argentina, South Africa and the Ukraine, who used the Conference to indicate their desire to be fully re-integrated into the society of states.

By these actions, the NPT's centrality was reaffirmed by great and lesser powers alike. But there was more to it: membership of and compliance with the Treaty was coming to be regarded as a precondition for membership of the society of states, a viewpoint that the United States among others was keen to advance. Hedley Bull wrote that:

> *a society of states (or international society) exists when a group of states, conscious of certain common interests and common values, form a society in the sense that they conceive themselves to be bound by a common set of rules in their rela-tions with one another, and share in the working of common institutions.*[5]

At its birth in the 1960s, the NPT was the child of a small group of states. By April 1995 when the Extension Conference convened, all but six states were represented, among which only three (Israel, India and Pakistan) remained defiantly opposed to membership. In consequence, the NPT appeared in the mid-1990s to be becoming the property and manifestation of a true international society – even a global society – of states.

Second, many Treaty members and especially the NNWS regarded the Extension Conference as a quasi-legislative assembly whose collective decisions would bind its members to a path towards complete nuclear disarmament via arms reductions and strengthened regulatory regimes. Belief that the society of NPT members was acquiring this guiding authority appeared to be confirmed by two of the three 'decisions' that accompanied the resolution extending the Treaty's lifetime. Those decisions entailed a provision for a strengthened review process allowing state parties to conduct more thorough and regular reviews of the Treaty's implementation; and the adoption of 20 Principles and Objectives by which member states would 'continue to move with determination towards the full realization and effective implementation of the provisions of the Treaty'.[6] They included a renewed commitment to achieve universal membership of the Treaty, the strongest statement yet enjoining states parties to pursue arms reductions and disarmament, a commitment to negotiate the CTBT and the Fissile Material Cut-off Treaty (FMCT), and an endorsement of efforts to reform IAEA safeguards.[7]

Third, these developments implied that the NPT had attained a strong and near universal legitimacy, with only India strongly challenging it from the outside. However, it was not an indefinite, unconditional legitimacy: it still depended on parties honouring their various commitments. Furthermore, at this height of legitimacy, increasing doubts emerged regarding the Treaty's efficacy, especially in connection with the absence of agreed mechanisms for responding to non-compliance. Indeed, there was concern that too great a preoccupation with upholding the Treaty's legitimacy could blind member states to the challenges that they faced, especially from states prepared to violate the Treaty in pursuit of nuclear weapons.

Although the NPT Review Conference in 2000 issued an even stronger statement with more precise proposals on disarmament (the Thirteen Steps), the 1995 Extension Conference marked the apogee of multilateralism in this field. The CTBT's negotiation was concluded in 1996 but its entry into force was immediately obstructed when India, taking advantage of an opportunity presented by the UK, refused to sign it.[8] The Canberra Commission on the Elimination of Nuclear Weapons reported in 1996 but was ignored. The safeguards reforms were approved in 1997 but ran into trouble over matters of implementation. Since then, it has been downhill most of the way. The Principles and Objectives today stand as a damaged monument to the cooperative aspirations of the early post-Cold War period, and the group of states that drafted them can no longer confidently call itself an international society by Hedley Bull's definition, let alone a global society of states uniting around common norms. The decisive blow to the idea that this society could operate a quasi-legislative assembly through the NPT conference and review processes came in 1999 when the US Senate rejected the CTBT, which had long been regarded as integral to the NPT and promoted by the US government itself.

Something else happened in the mid-1990s. The triumphs of cooperative politics represented by the successful reconstitution of the former Soviet Union and extension of the NPT gave the US greater confidence to 'lay down the definitive terms of the post-Cold War peace settlement'.[9] It felt freer to express its hegemonic aspirations and to ignore the demands of other powers (such as Russia's appeals over NATO expansion). The success of multilateralism thus ironically created the grounds for unilateralism. The shift towards hegemonic assertion was accompanied by the Republican Party's increasing dominance of Congress after the 1994 elections, and by growing disillusion with Russia, as its democratic and economic reforms faltered.[10] In Washington, the seeds of the later move against multilateralism were already being sown.

Path 2: Towards the coercive elimination of others' WMD

Robert Kagan has written that 'America did not change after 11 September 2001. It only became more itself'.[11] From the outside let alone the inside, Kagan's assertion is hard to accept. The United States did change after 11 September. Externally, the United States' relation to and respect for international order changed radically. Given its burgeoning hegemonic power and will, the effects on the international order – indeed on all international orders – was bound to be dramatic. The United States' view of and behaviour in the world will inevitably occupy centre stage in ensuing pages. This is not to claim that other states were unimportant or that the shift in US attitudes was generated just by internal factors. As usual, the outcome resulted from a complicated interplay of the external and the internal, and its effect on the ideas and interests that shaped policy.

The impact of 9/11 on international order was to dislodge finally the American commitment to an international ordering strategy that could combine power play with the enthusiastic development of constitutional norms and practices. It finally did so because although the commitment to this strategy had for reasons which will be explored below weakened in the years preceding 9/11, it always seemed possible, even after George W. Bush's election, that US policy would spring back to this familiar orthodoxy. After all, this is what happened during the Reagan presidency. After 9/11, however, a return to constitutionalism seemed less likely, especially concerning US handling of WMD threats.

Why did the commitment to the blend of constitutionalism and power play that had apparently served the United States so well weaken in the 1990s? In retrospect, the Gulf War of 1991 spurred forces that would later destabilise US policy. Five aspects of the war and its aftermath deserve to be highlighted, relating to perceptions of military preponderance, the fusion of weapons of mass destruction, the emergence of new routes to weapon acquisition, the focus on the Middle East, and the emergence of counter-proliferation policy, which is discussed in the following chapter.

The realisation of military preponderance

The Gulf War led to the United States' discovery of its military preponderance and of the scope for extending its military sway by exploiting the new information technologies in warfare.[12] As military actions in the Balkans, Afghanistan and Iraq were to demonstrate even more tellingly, the abilities of states (albeit minor powers in these cases) to conduct regular warfare against the United States were being reduced almost to vanishing point by technological advances. The technology gap was not transient: the 'Revolution in Military Affairs' (RMA) involved a progressive development and integration of technology systems that no other state or combination of states could be expected to match for a long time to come. Unlike the atomic bomb, this military capability appeared to provide the United States with a lead that could not be whittled away. In knowledge of their military inferiority, it was fair to assume that other states – including Russia and China – would increasingly be drawn into bandwagoning with the US if they wished to evade punishment. Unless, that is, they resorted to unconventional means of frustrating US hegemony or if that hegemony proved less overwhelming than anticipated.

Furthermore, the new technologies seemed to provide the United States with the capacity to wage war without significant risk to its military forces and with fewer civilian casualties on the ground.

This appeared to diminish the risk of mass casualties, a principal factor in de-legitimising war in previous decades, especially within the United States. As these trends were extrapolated into the future, the lesson from Vietnam that wars against even minor powers were unconscionable no longer seemed valid. The crucial proviso, to which we shall return, was that opposing states were deprived of WMD, which alone could inflict extensive injury or deter attack. Though the US was achieving an unmatchable supremacy in 'conventional' weapons, a more widespread diffusion of WMD could spoil its advantage.

The political fusion of WMD

The Gulf War triggered the re-connection of the three weapons of mass destruction (four if one includes ballistic missiles) and the raising of their combined political salience. They were fused by a realisation of Iraq's desire to obtain CBW and use them (in the case of chemical weapons) as instruments of internal repression against the Kurds and of warfare against Iran; by Iraq's implicit threat to use missiles armed with chemical weapons against Israel and US forces stationed in Saudi Arabia; by the United States' counter-threat of a retaliatory nuclear strike on Iraq; and by the increased focus on other Middle Eastern states' efforts to acquire CBW to deter Israel and other neighbouring states. The political reality of this fusion was displayed at the end of the Gulf War in UNSC Resolution 687, which gave equal priority to the elimination of Iraq's chemical, biological, nuclear and missile capabilities.

Together with the Soviet and then Russian government's acknowledgement of the enormous stocks of chemical munitions that had been amassed in the Cold War, these developments provided the impetus for negotiations on a global treaty banning the possession and use of chemical weapons, which became the Chemical Weapons Convention of 1993 (CWC). This treaty was followed in 1994 and ensuing years by an initiative to negotiate a protocol to the Biological and Toxin Weapons Convention of 1972 (BTWC), which would give it the instrument of verification that it lacked. Along with the efforts to reform nuclear safeguards and widen the reach of the nuclear and missile export-control systems, restraints on the diffusion of all of these weapons were therefore sought through multilateral and other processes. The important point was that progress in inhibiting the diffusion and preventing the use of *all* of the weapons of mass destruction would henceforth be deemed essential to international order. This conclusion came from both realist and idealist directions: realist in that power balances were now considered threatened by the acquisition of any of these weapons since each potentially attained deterrent value; idealist in that the goal of complete nuclear disarmament was now contingent upon chemical and biological disarmament, given that nuclear weapons were ostensibly needed to deter CBW attacks.

The technologies' obvious differences did not therefore prevent them from being grouped together at the political and strategic level into a single category – the weapon of mass destruction – which replaced the nuclear weapon as the main rhetorical signifier of outlandish threat. Indeed, just as the nuclear weapon appeared to be losing some of its salience in global politics, the adoption of this general term seemed to ensure a continuation and indeed magnification of outlandish threats and of the corollary and imperative need to refocus ordering strategies. As Janne Nolan has argued, it also helped institutions with stakes in nuclear weapons to frustrate calls for a more radical reduction of nuclear arms in the Nuclear Posture Review, which the US government had initiated in the early 1990s.[13]

Concerns were particularly focused on the behaviour of 'rogue states'.[14] These were states, prominent among them Iraq and North Korea, who had placed WMD at the centre of strategies for extending power and prestige or for ensuring survival, and who had 'cheated from within' by mounting covert weapon programmes in violation of treaty obligations. In so doing, they caused offence in Washington both to advocates of a constitutional order that required states to comply routinely and rigorously with international norms and laws, and to advocates of an overt hegemonic order in which the United States would use its enhanced military and economic power to ensure compliance with its will. Stripping rogue states of their capacities to threaten injury would thenceforth stand high among US security goals.

Processes of weapon acquisition: the procurement network
Iraq's defeat in the 2003 Gulf War revealed not just the scale of its weapon programmes, but also the extent of the international procurement activity that had made them possible and which had

gone largely undetected by verification and intelligence agencies. A certain model of weapon acquisition had previously been assumed: the proliferating state would probably stay outside the NPT to avoid safeguards and purchase whole facilities (reactors, reprocessing and/or enrichment plants) on the pretext that they were needed for civil purposes. It now became evident that a state could purchase the required components and sub-systems through a disguised network of suppliers located in various countries and assemble them into complete facilities.[15] Furthermore, the Iraqi programme revealed how European and North American universities had unwittingly provided Iraqi scientists and engineers with training relevant to weapon design and manufacture.

Hopes were pinned on the reforms of the safeguard and export-control systems noted above. It was nevertheless recognised that the march of economic globalisation could, along with the general diffusion of scientific and technological understandings, substantially reduce barriers to the acquisition of WMD. Furthermore, the problem could not be addressed only or even mainly through stricter international regulation. Timely detection would increasingly have to rely upon intelligence services acting in some form of collaboration with verification agencies. Furthermore, international control would have little chance of success if not accompanied by effective domestic regulation and the penalisation of transgressors. In turn, these realisations became entangled with concerns over the guardianship of the former Soviet Union's immense nuclear, chemical and biological weapon infrastructures. An external actor would only require access to a tiny proportion of its expertise and materiel to lay the foundations of a substantial weapons programme.

In all these respects, Iraq therefore provided a warning that capabilities could diffuse rapidly and remain undetected in the absence of heightened vigilance and tougher regulation within both the domestic and international spheres, a reality that would later be confirmed by the revelation of Abdul Qadeer Khan's Pakistan-based network. Moreover, the fusion of the weapons of mass destruction in the political and strategic consciousness meant that controls would have to be extended and strengthened across an increasingly wide field of science and technology, now including the burgeoning field of biotechnology. To some, this goal seemed unrealistic, especially in an environment in which many governments were prone to corruption and were struggling to exercise internal authority.

The Middle East: a Hobbesian realm of unbridled enmity

The Gulf War, the renewed concern over WMD, and Iraq and Iran's identification as 'rogue states' further solidified the US strategic preoccupation with the Middle East. Hitherto, US security analysts had been able to take Israel's nuclear monopoly almost for granted, given Egypt's renunciation of nuclear weapons in the early 1970s and the near universal membership of the NPT within the Middle East. For a brief period, the combination of the reinvigorated Middle East peace process following the Oslo accords, the dual containment of Iraq and Iran, the negotiation of the CWC and reinforcement of the NPT through the 1995 Extension Conference (which had adopted the Resolution on the Middle East in recognition of Arab concerns about Israel) seemed to open up possibilities for a security order that would remove WMD from the region.[16] But this was a fleeting moment.

There was an altogether darker view in Washington that this was a region of pure and unbridled enmity, a region inhabited by corrupt and anachronistic governments that did not share Western ideas of rational or moral behaviour, and where there was little respect for international constitutionalism or belief that it could bring the salvation claimed by its proponents. Furthermore, this was a region in which some political and religious leaders openly expressed not only the desire to destroy a state (Israel) and evict its people (the Jews), but also appeared intent on acquiring weapons that could make these threats tangible. The United States was ensnared in the region by oil, by its unshakeable devotion towards Israel and Saudi Arabia, and its equally unshakeable enmity towards Iran, Iraq, and Syria, an enmity reciprocated in full measure. From this viewpoint, peace was a mirage: the Middle East was irredeemably Hobbesian (or Schmittean) and immune to the kind of politics that held sway elsewhere. Furthermore, an elite in Washington, strongly influenced by its connections with Israel and the Middle East, was inclined to argue that this region revealed the essential nature of international politics. It was folly to base US security policy on an expectation that the cooperative ideals of the UN Charter, the EU or for that matter the NPT could be substantially realised at the global let alone regional level. In several ways, the Middle East replaced Central Europe and the Far East as the primary shaper of the United States' security mindset in the years following the end of the Cold War.

Chapter 4

The breakdown of WMD order

Although confidence in the prior nuclear order was eroding, its breakdown was not inevitable. It was precipitated in significant part by the emergence of powerful revisionist forces in two giant states: the US and India. India's revisionism was unsettling, but unlike that of the US did not constitute a fundamental challenge to the international order. The United States has always been a revisionist power insofar as it has constantly sought to revise the behaviour of other peoples and states. However, the nature of its revisionism changed markedly in two stages. First, the annus horribilis of 1998 brought a series of shocks that cast further doubt over the dominant US ordering strategies and enabled their critics to make substantial advances. These shocks – the Indian and Pakistani test explosions in May, the North Korean test of the *Taepo-Dong* missile in August, and the collapse of UNSCOM's mission in Iraq in December. Second, the arrival of the Bush administration in January 2001 and the profound disturbance of 11 September 2001 together moved US policy onto a radically new path.

Stage 1: 1998–2001
India and Pakistan's nuclear tests

India's nuclear programme has a long and complex history.[1] The motivation for crossing the threshold and deploying nuclear weapons after a long period of resisting such temptation was fundamentally revisionist. In the regional context, India wished to change the nature of its relations with China and Pakistan so as to balance Chinese power and assert hegemony in South Asia. This latter ambition was fuelled by unrest in Kashmir and the resurgence of

Hindu nationalism, which had brought the Bharatiya Janata Party (BJP) to power in April 1998. In the global context, India craved admission to the ranks of the great powers, a status granted to China, France, Russia, the UK and the US and institutionalised through the UNSC and NPT but denied to India. It thereby came to exhibit the double enmity referred to in Chapter 1: enmity against Pakistan and incipient enmity against China; and enmity against a constitutional order (especially as instituted in the NPT), which in India's opinion was locking it into a position of inferiority. This latter enmity was aggravated in the mid-1990s by the NPT Extension Conference, and by the explicit attempt to confine India's nuclear ambitions by coercing it into joining the CTBT.[2] India's tests were thus a strike against the constitutional order epitomised by the NPT as much as a move to alter power relations with other states.[3]

Although India's actions were not sufficient to destroy the nuclear order, they undoubtedly wounded it. They undermined the principle of universality that had been emphasised at the NPT Extension Conference; obstructed the entry into force of the CTBT and the negotiation of the FMCT; and damaged the NPT's prestige in the eyes of other leading states that had foresworn nuclear weapons. More generally, India's actions punctured the notion embedded in the NPT that nuclear history would comprise a once-and-for-all expansion of nuclear arms followed by a contraction leading asymptotically to zero. Furthermore, the tests initially seemed to heighten rather than diminish the enmity between India and Pakistan. Indeed, as the conflict in Kashmir intensified, diplomatic relations were severed, and there was justifiable concern about the fallibility of deterrence given the short distances involved, the absence of early warning systems and the abundance of political tripwires. Rather than reduce enmity to a manageable rivalry, the nuclear and missile tests appeared to aggravate it.

Taepo-Dong, missile defence and the critique of deterrence

In August 1998, North Korea launched a multi-stage rocket over the Sea of Japan (East Sea). The *Taepo-Dong* test aroused acute concern in Japan over its vulnerability to North Korean blackmail and over its potential humiliation by a state and people that it had traditionally held in low regard. Within the United States, the North Korean missile test intensified criticism of the Agreed Framework, the deal struck in 1994 by the US and North Korean governments under which North Korea would freeze and then dismantle its weapon programme in return for various benefits. Equally significantly, it provided timely ammunition for proponents of missile defence. As in the 1980s, increasingly influential critics of nuclear deterrence underlined the necessity of missile defence: although deterrence may have worked in the Cold War, they argued, it could not be relied upon to constrain 'irrational actors' whose calculations might be very different from those of the US.[4] Furthermore, the risk-aversion of Western democracies meant that 'rogue states' armed with a handful of WMD might be able to deter rather than be deterred, despite US military superiority.

The *Taepo-Dong* test appeared to validate the Rumsfeld Report to the US Congress of July 1998, which had claimed that Iran and North Korea, held as the ultimate irrational actors, would soon be able to threaten the US mainland with warhead-bearing missiles.[5] Calls for the construction of a national missile defence quickly gathered pace leading to the US Congress' passage of the National Missile Defense Act in July 1999.[6] This decision aggravated relations between the US, Russia and China, and between the US and its allies in Europe, as it challenged both the ABM Treaty and the system of nuclear deterrence developed over the previous half century. To American opponents of the ABM Treaty, its abrogation would enable the United States to use its formidable technological capacities to develop an unmatchable strategic advantage over future rivals (prominently China), regain invulnerability to external threat, and end the anachronistic maintenance of parity with a weakened Russia. What excited the ABM Treaty's opponents appeared dangerous to its supporters: national missile defence would encourage the militarisation of space and jeopardise the 'strategic stability' that had long underpinned relations between the great powers. Deep down, the argument was over the kind of international order that would prevail in future: the establishment of a condominium of great powers, or a shift to a more naked form of hegemony.

UNSCOM's demise

The breakdown of UNSCOM in December 1998 marked the culmination of a chain of events stretching back several years.

Whatever successes the UN had achieved, it became increasingly hard to avoid the conclusion that an obstinate government could always hinder the complete elimination of its WMD programmes, especially where CBW were concerned. Furthermore, the UNSC could not carry out such a delicate task with divisions among its members. Iraq's compliance with Resolution 687 had come to rely upon the threat of military action. This threat became harder to sustain through the UNSC, as China, Russia and other states perceived military intervention in the Balkans, Iraq and elsewhere as whittling away the norms of state sovereignty.

Thus Iraq seemed to highlight a fundamental flaw in the 'system of abstinence' just as it was claimed to be rendering unreliable any 'system of deterrence'. Although the norm of non-proliferation was deeply entrenched, there was no reliable mechanism for dealing with states that defied it. This was fertile ground in which to plant the seeds of a different approach. A now famous letter of 26 January 1998 from 18 figures on the American political right called upon President Bill Clinton 'to enunciate a new strategy', which 'should aim, above all, at the removal of Saddam Hussein's regime from power' without the Security Council's support if need be.[7] 'American policy cannot continue to be crippled by a misguided insistence on unanimity in the UN Security Council.'[8] Whilst the letter's proposals did not become official US policy for another four years, the credibility in Washington of the UN-centred approach to non-compliance had by the time of its writing already begun to erode.

The emergence of counter-proliferation

In retrospect, three American actions in 1998 and in 1999 were portents of the dramatic shift in the US ordering strategy that occurred in the first years of the twenty-first century. On 16 December 1998, the American and British governments launched *Operation Desert Fox* without UNSC consent and bombed Iraq's WMD sites, ostensibly in response to the failure of cooperative disarmament. By so doing, the United States indicated its loss of patience with diplomatic processes and its preparedness to take military action against a proliferating state without the imprimatur of international legitimacy. Counter-proliferation, which had been inaugurated by the Department of Defense in 1993–94 but initially kept on the margins of US security policy, was gaining ascendancy over non-proliferation.[9] Then in July 1999, as we have seen, the US Congress enacted the National Missile Defense Act in defiance of the administration. This was followed in November 1999 by the US Senate's decisive rejection of the CTBT. Whatever the causes of the Clinton administration's failure to secure the Treaty's ratification, the Congressional decisions confirmed what was already apparent: that the United States was turning away from the multilateral treaty-bound route to international order wherever it placed constraints on US freedom of action or to respond decisively to breaches of compliance.

In hindsight, the unexpected agreement on the ambitious Final Document at the NPT Review Conference in May 2000 was a last ditch attempt to stem the tide. The Document committed all state parties (the United States included) to uphold two principles: a principle of irreversibility and a principle of completion. The former would ensure full compliance with established arms control, arms reduction and disarmament measures. The latter would finalise measures singled out for development (notably the CTBT and FMCT) and pursue the project of disarmament with greater vigour through the Thirteen Steps.[10]

These principles held little appeal to a Republican-dominated US Congress or to the incoming Bush administration, possessed as it was by a desire to move the United States away from multilateralism.[11] The new administration quickly abandoned the blend of constitutionalism, power balancing and hegemony that had marked policy since America's emergence as a world power in the 1940s. Instead, it called upon the United States to use its military and economic supremacy to 'shape a new century', to create such an impregnable advantage that no other state could hope to challenge or constrain its leadership, and in so doing, to free itself from the encumbrance of multilateralism.[12] Within a few months of his entering the White House, President Bush had presided over an enormous increase in defence spending, pressed ahead with the funding of missile defence and abrogation of the ABM Treaty, abandoned the principle of verification in arms reductions, and indicated that he was prepared to 'unsign' the CTBT in the national interest. Furthermore, the administration had done its best to destroy the BTWC Protocol and the process by which it had been negotiated, and had moved against the Kyoto Protocol, the International Criminal Court and various other multilateral initiatives.

Although entrenched and given a radical twist by 9/11, the shift in US policy therefore preceded the attacks on the Twin Towers. Its grounds were laid by the above-mentioned trends and events, which nourished a critique of – and enmity towards – prior ordering strategies. The critique involved, among other things, an attack on the core assumptions that had underpinned the systems of deterrence and abstinence, and was used to justify movement towards a system of self-protection and enforced abstinence. Taken together, these trends and events fed and were fed by an increasingly dystopian American view of the outside world. It drew on an increasing sense of difference and loss of trust in sameness, of disaffection and disorientation, of a tangible vulnerability to attack, of alone having to carry the costs of maintaining order following the Soviet Union's demise. In just one short decade, a long journey was travelled from 'the new international order' and Fukuyama's *End of History* to Huntington's *Clash of Civilizations* to Kagan's *Of Paradise and Power*.[13] Each in its distinctive way offered a redefinition of the relationship between the Self and the Other. For Fukuyama, there was little need to worry, as all Others were coming to resemble the neo-liberal American Self. For Huntington, there was every reason to worry, as the Others were irredeemably different and could not be made to resemble the Self (for down that coercive road lay disaster). For Kagan, similarities and differences did not matter, as Others could and should be driven into subservience by the exercise of imperial might. Although these were just three among countless texts, they expressed a journey shared by many Americans from one certainty through anxiety towards another certainty, however fleeting that return to certainty might turn out to be. By tapping deeply into American anxiety about the external world, 9/11 enabled Huntington's anxious caution to be replaced if only briefly by Kagan's brash incaution.

Stage 2: 2001–03
Catastrophic terrorism and international order

By definition, a non-state actor is not a member of the society of states. Most non-state actors (such as firms and NGOs) abide by the norms and rules established by states and may play a constructive part in shaping them. There is however a set of non-state actors that resort to violence against a state or states because the latter embody a status quo that they wish to overthrow. Such actors, which include terrorist groups, partisans and guerrilla fighters, are always branded illegitimate by their target states. They have no intrinsic right to exist, allowing states to claim unchallengeable rights to retaliate and destroy in self-defence. This is the realm of true enmity and, in extremity, of the absolute enmity alluded to by Carl Schmitt in his *Theorie des Partisanen*.

Conflicts involving non-state actors are marked by asymmetries of capabilities and of constraint in their use. In most cases, the state enjoys greater resources and majority backing, forcing its opponent to choose means and targets deemed abhorrent. This very abhorrence provokes societies, governments and media to magnify the injury, thereby creating the mass effect aimed for by the terrorist. Nonetheless, the typical terrorist group does not operate totally without restraint. It may be restrained by the paucity of its capabilities, the need to conduct its operations from the shadows and the desire not to antagonise constituencies that may be attracted to its cause.

WMD, as traditionally defined, have not been regarded as weapons of choice for non-state actors, as they require a high level of technological expertise and cause a level of damage that might seriously endanger support for whichever group attempted to use them.[14] In the late 1990s, however, a debate emerged over the possibility that terrorist groups might shed this restraint and perpetrate acts of 'catastrophic terrorism' using nuclear, chemical or biological weapons.[15] A series of terrorist attacks in the 1990s, including the attempted destruction of the World Trade Center in 1992, Aum Shinrikyo's release of sarin in the Tokyo subway in 1995 and the bomb blasts in Oklahoma, Moscow and Dar es Salaam, pointed towards an increasing willingness among some terrorist groups to cause mass casualties in service of political, ideological or religious ends. Furthermore, the US was becoming a primary focus of this enmity, as typified by Osama bin Laden's 'declaration of war' against it in 1996.[16]

Within the United States, a burgeoning literature expressed growing concerns that the US homeland and US forces and interests abroad could be targeted, that under-protected infrastructures in

Russia were providing unprecedented access to WMD materiel and expertise, and that a substantial WMD attack could have terrible consequences for society and its confidence in government. Ashton Carter and William Perry made this prescient observation in 1999:

> *An incident of catastrophic terrorism would abruptly and irrevocably undermine the fundamental sense of security of Americans, their belief that the United States is a safe place to live, to make plans, to raise a family … For the most part in American experience, security threats have arisen in faraway places, and the violence has taken place there. Catastrophic terrorism would bring the national security threat home again. The result would be profoundly disturbing to Americans.*[17]

Although the type of attack that occurred on 11 September 2001 was not foreseen, there had been prior speculation about the risks arising from a more vigorous brand of international terrorism. That speculation extended into the intelligence services, armed forces and civil agencies, which increasingly found themselves having to take precautionary measures against terrorist attack (preparations for the Atlanta Olympics in 1996 having a galvanising effect). Until 9/11, however, the risks were too uncertain and incalculable to provide impetus for a fundamental shift in US attitudes and policies. To quote Carter and Perry:

> *Like an attack on Pearl Harbor, an incident of catastrophic terrorism would divide our past and future into "before" and "after". The effort and resources we have so far devoted to averting or containing this threat now, in the period "before", would seem woefully inadequate when viewed with hindsight after an incident of catastrophic terrorism.*[18]

The attack on the Twin Towers provided that moment when, for the United States, political time would be divided into the before and the after. In the after, international terrorism would be portrayed as the greatest challenge to America's predominance and international order.

Al-Qaeda did not use WMD in their attacks on New York and Washington. They turned civilian airliners into weapons of mass effect in their truest sense. The 11 September attacks thus demonstrated that a weapon of mass destruction is not needed to inflict enormous political and psychological injury on a great power. An advanced industrial society offers a wide range of inviting targets to those with the requisite skill, imagination and ruthlessness.[19] Yet regardless of how they may have been viewed by terrorist groups, the weapon of mass destruction became the ultimate terrorist weapon in the imagination of its potential victims. If used effectively, it might cause death, injury and disruption on a scale dwarfing the attack on the Twin Towers. To governments, the usage of such a weapon was the stuff of nightmares, creating a situation in which it would be hard to exert control and avoid a dramatic loss of confidence in political leaders and institutions. In the imagination of governments and their leaders, such weapons could indeed become 'destroyers of worlds' to recall Robert Oppenheimer's comment about the atomic bomb in 1945.

This realisation gave rise to a new but perilous three-part security logic:

1.   The threat from terrorist groups armed with, or arming them-selves with, a weapon of mass destruction (of whichever kind) is intolerable. Assuming that such groups are committed to surprise attack and prepared to inflict mass casualties, and that they are largely 'undeterrable', they have to be found and destroyed. Neither their containment nor the protection of society against their attack can suffice. The Other has to be destroyed, and destroyed soon, if the Self is to survive.

2.   The threat from such groups is magnified if they are support-ed by regimes that provide them with shelter and/or access to materials, expertise and other resources. In so doing, such regimes place themselves beyond the pale: they forfeit their rights to recognition and survival. They too invite their own destruction.

3.   States that provide no succour to international terrorists but do not accept this security logic will fail the test of international collegiality and be made to suffer accordingly. 'Those who are not with us, are against us.'[20]

This logic appeared compelling. The end of the Cold War had raised the US to a position of dominance in the international system that had few parallels in history. Yet, in the American mind, it was a highly vulnerable dominance. Missile defence, counter-proliferation and counter-terrorism – the new commanding heights of US security policy – all centred on regaining invulnerability in the face of a creeping malevolence and disorder. In this mood, containment would no longer suffice, and constitutionalism was meaningless if it provided no absolute security. Faced with this overwhelming sense of dystopia and an unprecedented belief in the superior virtue of the American people and state, the preferred option was to call upon US power and pride, take the fight to the enemy and gain lasting security by transforming the polities from which it emerged.

The US National Security Strategy of 2002

Viewed from the outside, the 'war on terrorism' and the increasingly vociferous calls for war against Iraq were deeply ambiguous in intent. It was not clear where the boundaries lay between justifiable self-defence and a programme of imperial expansion. The new security imperative carried with it the temptation for a hegemonic power to seize the moment to extend its military reach and recast the international order in its self-interest. The intent seemed to become unambiguous in that extraordinary document of September 2002, the National Security Strategy of the USA.[21] This was more than a strategy for defeating international terrorism and managing a more complex post-Cold-War environment. It was a charter, certainly as seen from abroad, confirming America's hegemonic status and propagating 'a distinctly American internationalism that reflects the union of our values and our national interest'.[22] The question of order posed by the emergence of new lethal threats was thus enmeshed with the question of order posed by the emergence of an assertive United States.

Several aspects of this new international strategy and the thinking behind it, as displayed in the National Security Strategy, deserve attention. First, it re-emphasised the primacy of obligation towards the American Self, and asserted that this and no other Self had an untrammelled right to define its interests and to decide on the means of promoting them (the trend to unilateralism). According to the National Security Strategy, this should not bring conflict with Others since the Self's interests and ideals were the Others' enlightened interests and ideals. Assertive hegemony thus went hand in hand with a revitalised emphasis on American exceptionalism.

Second, the United States had the freedom and right to express enmity and amity towards other states, even to nominate its friends and enemies, encouraged as it was by the inability of any other state to force enmity's reduction to a balanced rivalry. This was tantamount to removing the middle ground between enmity and amity in the schema depicted in Figure 1. Indeed, the price of rivalry, especially if sought through the acquisition of WMD, would be an unquenchable enmity that could place the very survival of the hostile state or regime in jeopardy. When President Bush asserted that 'states like these, and their terrorist allies, constitute an axis of evil' in his State of the Union address in 2002, he was also signalling that such actors had no right on their side and were irredeemable through normal political action ('we are in a conflict between good and evil, and America will call evil by its name').[23]

Third, the National Security Strategy expounded a stance on constitutionalism that placed freedom of the Self above collective deliberation and restraint (even to the extent of abrogating instruments of mutual restraint such as the ABM Treaty); marginalised the UN and its related institutions (the document mentions the UN only once and then tangentially in connection with the financing of development); selectively used international laws and regimes to bind other states to patterns of behaviour which served the hegemonic interest; and justified coercive actions against states that defied that interest. This was thus a multilateralism stripped of reciprocal obligation and collective decision-making. According to this doctrine, the United States – rather than the UN Security Council – would henceforth determine the boundaries between international legitimacy and illegitimacy.

Fourth, the National Security Strategy looked forward to a new era of cooperative relations between the United States and other great powers in confronting the terrorist threat. It speaks of setting aside old animosities in order to establish 'a new strategic relationship' with Russia, 'a constructive relationship with China' and 'a strong relationship with India'.[24] Envisaged was a coalition of powers organised and led by the United States. It was explicitly stated that 'our forces will be strong enough to dissuade potential adversaries from pursuing a military build-up in hopes of surpassing, or equaling, the power of the United States'.[25] The message was clear: US power could not and would not be balanced. Bandwagoning was the only option available to other great powers if they were to avoid the sharp sting of US displeasure.

Fifth, the National Security Strategy and its accompanying National Strategy to Combat Weapons of Mass Destruction of December 2002 completed the fusion of nuclear, chemical and biological weapons into the single category 'WMD'. The acquisition or usage by an enemy of any of these weapons or their constituent parts, in whichever quantity or quality, would justify decisive action. The strategy to reduce the threat from WMD would henceforth rest on three pillars – counter-proliferation, non-proliferation and consequence management – with priority given to the first and last. Through 'targeted strategies against proliferants', pressure would be 'brought to bear ... against states of WMD proliferation concern, as well as against terrorist groups which seek to acquire WMD'.[26] There was heavy emphasis throughout the document on coercion with little evident desire to persist with the patient inducement that had been pursued through non-proliferation policy. Indeed, impatience colours the entire National Security Strategy, most controversially in the declared willingness to act pre-emptively against transgressors. 'To forestall or prevent such hostile acts by our adversaries, the United States will, if necessary, act preemptively.'[27]

Lastly, democratisation and market liberalisation were perceived as the keys towards 'decades of peace, prosperity, and liberty'.[28] A stable international order would follow the adoption of democratic and liberal economic practices by all states of whichever size and culture. This is an old American theme, but the vigorous idealism animating it was freshly minted. Michael Mazarr has written of the 'utopian, transformative language' used by the Bush administration to express its essential idealism.[29] 'What is at stake is not just America's freedom. This is the world's fight. This is civilization's fight. This is the fight of all who believe in progress and pluralism, tolerance and freedom.'[30]

The National Security Strategy was a rhetorical device intended primarily for a domestic audience in the aftermath of 9/11. This said, it was the declared security strategy of the United States and bound to be read as such by foreign audiences. Furthermore, its very orientation towards a domestic audience implied insensitivity to foreign interests, opinions and reactions. In selecting this approach, the United States risked jeopardising its ability to create global order and paved the way for imperial overstretch. If the US had instead emphasised the centrality of international law and the international constitutional framework together with the necessity of reinforcing albeit adapting them to changed circumstances, the outcome could have been very different. By so visibly turning against the constitutional order, it lost international goodwill and reduced its capacity to bring other states and peoples into the fold. As Joseph Nye has written, 'if we [Americans] squander our soft power through a combination of arrogance and indifference, we will increase our vulnerability, sell our values short, and hasten the erosion of our pre-eminence'.[31] In the WMD context, the US risked sacrificing both the efficacy and legitimacy of the international order that it had gone to such pains to establish in previous years.

Chapter 5

The Iraq War and afterwards

There was a direct line from the National Security Strategy of 2002 to the war with Iraq, fought, ostensibly, on the grounds that the Iraqi regime was acquiring WMD, that it was seeking them for aggressive purposes, and that it had links with terrorist groups. The course of the war and the events that surrounded it – the fractious debates in the UNSC, the quick military victories of the US and its coalition partners, the failure to locate any significant WMD capabilities, and the gathering insurgency against the occupiers of Iraq – are well known and need not be repeated here.[1] The discussion will instead focus on the extent and limits of US power revealed by the war and its aftermath, on the subsequent behaviour of other 'rogue states' and implications for Pakistan, Saudi Arabia and Israel, and on the legitimacy and integrity of international institutions and actions in the wake of the war. In each respect, the situation is paradoxical and imbued with both opportunity and danger.

The revealed extent of and limits to US power

The Afghan and Iraq campaigns further demonstrated the extent of US military supremacy. The RMA has indeed provided the US with an unmatchable capacity to destroy the ability of minor powers (and possibly of some major powers) to engage it in regular warfare. However, as Iraq graphically illustrates, defeating a state in war and destroying its governing regime is a long distance from replacing them with a state and regime that are stable and well disposed towards the victor. Since the end of the Iraq War, the United States and its coalition partners have struggled to quell an insurgency and avoid the country's political fragmentation. As Mark Danner wrote:

The irony … is that while Saddam Hussein has been unseated, the threat that Iraq posed to the Gulf has not been removed. Indeed, it may be that the United States, with its overwhelming military power, has succeeded only in transforming an eventual and speculative threat into a concrete and immediate one.[2]

The past several months have shown that the idealism of the National Security Strategy was misplaced. Whatever view is taken of the legitimacy of preventive war, its credibility as a political strategy depends heavily on the ability to create a situation in the enemy state and its region that is clearly superior, in security terms, to that preceding it. The assumption that democracy is latent in all societies, that democratic processes carrying confidence will emerge once tyranny is overthrown, and that amity will replace enmity have been shown to be optimistic at best. Not only are the occupying powers struggling to establish political order within Iraq, the United States' authority and self-confidence also risk being damaged by its evident lack of control and by the impulse to retreat or garrison itself in the face of casualties and disorder. As in Vietnam, the domestic legitimacy of war can quickly erode if it does not achieve its stated aims, especially if the decision to go to war founded upon premises that turn out to be false. The decisions of the newly-elected Spanish government after the Madrid bombings illustrate that the same applies to the United States' coalition partners.

How the situation will develop in Iraq is unpredictable. Some are warning of state collapse and civil war, even of a wider upheaval involving Saudi Arabia and other states in the region. Others (increasingly in the minority) predict a gradual stabilisation as the economy and polity settle. Come what may, it will be difficult for the US, the UK or any other state to garner domestic and international support for another preventive war on WMD grounds unless the threat is accepted to be truly substantial, imminent and avoidable only by military means. Furthermore, everyone will now be aware that launching military actions in volatile regions where there is an abundance of political, ethnic and religious animosity risks provoking an even greater enmity against the invading powers and drawing them into a battleground advantageous to their opponents.

With regard to WMD, the US can now rest assured that this particular 'rogue state' can no longer, as a militarised state, threaten its vital interests. Regarding the first inter-state dimension of enmity discussed in Chapter 1, a potential rival has been removed. As for the second dimension of enmity, involving non-state actors, there can be no such certainty. In the political environment that has developed since the war ended in Iraq, the incentives for groups such as al-Qaeda to use a weapon of mass destruction of some kind may have increased.[3] Glory could come from striking a powerful state with the most feared weapon, and there may be a calculation that such an act would do more than anything else to unnerve publics and impel the United States to behave in the irregular ways that will serve the insurgents' interests. However, the opposite could also apply. Insurgent groups may consider it unnecessary to resort to WMD when there is so much opportunity to wound their enemy by other means. Furthermore, they may judge that any use of WMD could give the US and its allies greater resolve and authority to defeat them and thus widen the front against them.

No one can tell where the preference may lie. Nor can states be sure of the extant capabilities of the insurgent groups. Whatever conclusion may be drawn, governments are bound to assume that the threat exists and could be imminent. In this respect, the situation remains unchanged by the defeat of Iraq. Subsequent behaviour shows that governments are now bound to invest heavily in 'homeland security' and remain committed to the disruption and destruction of the international networks through which weapons may be assembled and acts of violence perpetrated. If anything, governments are likely to become even less tolerant of states acquiring WMD and trading in the materials, technologies and expertise. The threat and its accompanying anxiety are here to stay.

North Korea, Iran and Libya … and Pakistan, Saudi Arabia and Israel

The Iraq War was a perilous adventure. It is also evident, however, that the threat of preventive war or, more tellingly, of regime change has had a significant effect on the behaviour of other 'rogue states'. But the reactions have not been uniform. For North Korea, threat has been met with counter-threat.[4] It has rushed to develop and deploy a credible nuclear deterrent, or has at least endeavoured to send a strong message that this is now its objective. To achieve it, North Korea has removed itself from the NPT, evicted the IAEA inspectors, abrogated the Agreed Framework, and advertised its programmes for producing enriched uranium and plutonium. The perceived US threat of regime change, which could only be interpreted in Pyongyang as a threat to destroy the North Korean state through war, has created precisely the situation that the international community had hoped to avoid.

In this instance, aggressive counter-proliferation has encouraged proliferation. It has also increased China's role in the quest for a solution just as it has diminished the United States' influence over the outcome. It is now recognised that China has to be engaged; given its determination to safeguard its sphere of influence and its worries about consequences for Taiwan, Beijing will oppose any outcome that does not guarantee North Korea's survival. Any solution short of devastating war will therefore have to be multilateral and diplomatic. This is the clear implication of the Six-Party Talks presided over by China.

Iran's response has been different, although how different is not yet clear.[5] Fearful of the consequences of its inclusion in President Bush's 'axis of evil', it may initially have intended to follow North Korea's example by revealing and accelerating its weapon programme. Iran changed its policy following the Iraq War and the revelation of several facilities including its enrichment plant at Natanz. It has now acknowledged the existence of its nuclear activities, albeit whilst proclaiming their civil purpose, and has signed the Additional Protocol, which, if fully implemented, will substantially increase the IAEA's rights of access to sites and to design information.

Although Iran has doubtlessly been discomforted by US military encirclement following the wars in Afghanistan and Iraq, fears of imminent internal destabilisation may have been the more important reason for the Iranian government's initially cooperative approach. Having strengthened their hold on power, however, the conservative forces have recently seemed less prepared to comply with the IAEA and other demands to the extent of restarting the production of centrifuges for an enrichment programme. Throughout 2004, the IAEA, European Union, US and other players have struggled to hold Iran to its international commitments and to find a common response in the face of Iranian obduracy If Iran does not fully comply with its obligations, it may be just a matter of time before the issue is referred to the UN Security Council at which point it will become a serious test of whether international unity can be recovered after the Iraqi debacle.

Here again the US has found itself forced into an increasing reliance on other states (notably France, Germany and the UK acting in unison) and institutions (notably the IAEA), resulting in a consequent loss of control over the outcome. The same applies to Libya. Notwithstanding the role that US intelligence played in revealing the Libyan programme, the US government has had to concede a leading diplomatic role to the UK and a leading role in Libya's nuclear and chemical disarmament to the IAEA and the Organisation for the Prohibition of Chemical Weapons (OPCW).

One year after the Iraq War, two 'rogue states' in the Middle East and North Africa have therefore been removed from the roster of primary security threats to the US and its allies (if only in regard to their possession of WMD) or brought to a position (in Iran's case) where the threats may, if only temporarily, be more effectively contained. This shifts the spotlight onto states historically allied to and protected by the US: Pakistan, Saudi Arabia and Israel. Where Pakistan is concerned, there has already been substantial movement. Beginning with its government's decision to ally itself with the United States against the Taliban and al-Qaeda, Pakistan has also retreated from brinkmanship over Kashmir and sought to stabilise relations with India. In addition, Pakistan has acknowledged that its leading nuclear scientist had played a major part in transferring enrichment technology to Iran, Libya and North Korea, although concerns remain over the Pakistani government and security services' relationship to Khan's network. Trapped in hostility since attaining independence in 1947, it may be too much to expect that India and Pakistan will make a permanent transition to forbearance and amity, but a more controlled rivalry supported by nuclear deterrence may now be in prospect.

The extent of Saudi Arabia's involvement with WMD may not have been fully revealed. It is known that it has acquired ballistic missiles and provided financial assistance to Pakistan. There may be more to be discovered.[6] Saudi Arabia's greater significance lies in our second dimension of enmity – as a locus of the ideologies, grievances and animosities that have spurred the development of radical Islamist movements, with the Saudi regime being a principal target.

Its fate is beyond the scope of this Paper. Suffice to say that it is hard to imagine a durable peace in the Middle East without a fairly fundamental recasting of Saudi Arabia's polity and economy.

From the beginning of its nuclear programme in the 1960s, Israel has gone to extraordinary lengths to keep its nuclear weapons and strategies out of the public eye (this is the policy of opacity discussed by Avner Cohen).[7] Israel has nevertheless been at or near the epicentre of the crisis over WMD since the early 1990s, for reasons that take us back to the problem of enmity. It has found itself exposed to each of the three types of enmity identified by Carl Schmitt: the conventional enmity of states opposing states; the true enmity of insurgency, terrorism and irregular warfare; and the absolute enmity of actors dedicated to the destruction of Israel and expulsion of the Jewish people from Palestine. Furthermore, these various enmities have combined to produce state-terrorist connections, which have heightened Israel's insecurity and raised the prospect of irregular attacks by groups (including states) using WMD. The resort to suicide bombing has only added to the Israeli people's acute sense of vulnerability.

Viewed from other sides, Israel has been a principal driver of enmity of every kind in the Middle East, and a principal driver of quests for WMD. Although some of the weapon programmes have been fuelled by other states' ambitions and enmities (Iraq and Iran being particular examples), Israel's nuclear capability and supremacy in conventional weapons have encouraged and legitimised WMD proliferation within the region. Where unable to gain access to nuclear technology, states have turned to CBW instead, thereby reinforcing the link between the three weapons of mass destruction discussed earlier. More widely, the Islamic enmity against Israel and the United States has been inflamed by the aggressive tactics and expansionist aims of recent Israeli governments, which have created fertile ground for recruitment to radical groups prepared to use extreme violence. With far-reaching consequences, Israel has thus been involved, as victim and instigator, in the emergence of the threats that have radicalised US policy and fed its disdain for constitutional approaches to international order.

Establishing 'normality' in political practices and relations in the Middle East is of course an enormously difficult task. It has usually been assumed that the problems associated with Israel's

WMD can only begin to be addressed after success in a peace process, a success that in the last few years has seemed a distant prospect. However, the positive moves towards dismantling or constraining Libya and Iran's weapon programmes, along with the acknowledgment of Iraq's disarmament, may challenge this assumption. The consolidation of Iran's disarmament and the reining in of Syria and Egypt's CBW programmes may now hang on Israeli concessions. It is becoming increasingly difficult to justify the marginalisation of the long-advocated proposal to establish a WMD-free Middle East. As this proposal underlay the 1995 Resolution on the Middle East, it is likely to loom large at next year's NPT Review Conference.

The nature of these Israeli concessions remains to be seen. It has long been this author's view that Israel could be the last state to contemplate abandoning its nuclear deterrent, given the profound history-laden insecurities of the Jewish people. However those insecurities have been increased by the presence of WMD in the Middle East and the spectre of their usage. Some middle ground needs to be found that enables Israel to retain its guarantee of survival and satisfies other states' desires for security and equity of treatment. There are also increasingly insistent calls for Israel to abandon its policy of ambiguity so as to join India and Pakistan in developing a cooperative relationship with the non-proliferation regime.[8] Come what may, the status quo is becoming less sustainable.

Back to the problem of legitimacy

It is easy to be pessimistic about the diffusion of WMD. The past six years have seen the emergence of three nuclear powers (India, Pakistan and North Korea), the realisation that another state (Iran) had embarked on an ambitious programme of armament, and a deepening worry that terrorist groups might try to use CBW. Furthermore, the recent unearthing of the supply network that fed the Iranian, Libyan and North Korean enrichment programmes has shown that there are routes to acquisition that the best verification and intelligence agencies will always struggle to reveal.

The pessimism can, however, be overdone. Each state that has recently crossed the threshold to armament began its weapon programme 20 or more years ago. Moreover, the problem is still largely confined to three regions (the Middle East, South and North-

East Asia) and most states continue to display little appetite for any of the weapons of mass destruction. Finally, the nature of weapon programmes and the routes to acquisition can now be understood with greater clarity and it remains debatable whether non-state actors have the desire or ability to use WMD (at least in their most lethal forms).[9]

Whatever levels of pessimism or optimism may be justified, it is accepted that significant innovations will be required if a wider proliferation of WMD is to be averted. Some of the policy initiatives will be touched on below. However, identifying new policy measures, vital though they may be, and taking steps to develop them is not sufficient. Nor does concentration on the 'problem of proliferation' reveal anything like the full extent of the malaise. For the problem of WMD order is much more than the problem of WMD proliferation and of deficiencies in the instrumental means of addressing it. Nor is it just a problem of efficacy, meaning the capacity to deliver security. It is fundamentally a problem of efficacy *and* legitimacy and of their combined and mutually reinforcing achievement. It is the weakening of international legitimacy – even amounting to a crisis of legitimacy – that seems to present the gravest issue now confronting states and the state system.

A passage from Henry Kissinger's *A World Restored* deserves quotation:

> *There are two ways of constructing an international order …*
> *by conquest or by legitimacy … The difference between a rev-*
> *olutionary order and a healthy legitimate one is not the possi-*
> *bility of change, but the mode of its accomplishment. A "legit-*
> *imate" order … achieves its transformations through accept-*
> *ance, and this presupposes a consensus on the nature of a just*
> *arrangement. But a revolutionary order having destroyed the*
> *existing structure of obligations … must impose its measures*
> *by force … The health of a social structure is its ability to*
> *translate transformation into acceptance, to relate the forces of*
> *change to those of conservatism.*[10]

Three observations are in place. First, Kissinger's subject was in this instance the achievement of a settlement by Austria, Britain, Prussia, Russia and France after the defeat of Napoleon. For any 'legitimate order' to survive and prosper after its foundation, however, it has to be worked on and constantly reaffirmed. It has to grow and keep growing, and it is through its growth and the institutional creativity accompanying it that legitimacy and efficacy and thus order are maintained. This can be observed in the history of the EU, as in the development of the nuclear order from the 1950s into the 1990s. Any legitimate order will stagnate, its legitimacy and efficacy draining away, if its growth and creativity are halted and if its principal architects withdraw their commitment.

Second, the attainment of legitimacy within the nuclear order – and indeed within the international order as it developed in the twentieth century – had to be achieved on two levels simultaneously: among the great powers of the day, and among the broad community of states. As we have seen, this inherently complex task was addressed in the nuclear field through the highlighting and expansion of commitments to international norms – such as the norms of reciprocal obligation, non-proliferation and disarmament – and through the 'bargains' incorporated in the NPT.

Third, Kissinger was discussing a settlement sought among five great powers. Faced with intrinsic multipolarity, there was systemic pressure on them to attend to the issue of legitimacy. Order depended upon a shared respect for legitimacy and a shared perception of the order's legitimacy. The same applied during the Cold-War bi-polar balance of power. In a unipolar system, that systemic pressure is absent. The hegemon has a choice. It can create order through the coercive power upon which it confers its own legitimacy, in which case the order is no longer a *legitimate* order (it becomes an imperial order which is different). Alternatively, it can create order through power that is reined in yet augmented by international legitimacy. The final option is to strive for some persuasive combination of these two approaches.

As seen, the United States strove in the immediate post-Cold-War years to establish an order possessing extensive international legitimacy. But the US swung against this approach in the later 1990s and moved to abandon it in 2001 in favour of hegemonic coercion. In the process, the usually healthy rivalry within the United States between the different conceptions of order was overthrown. Those taking office in 2001 brought with them an antagonism towards constitutionalism and the very idea of an international legitimacy arrived at through cooperative diplomacy. As such, they assigned themselves autocratic rights and powers to diminish the sway of constitutionalism and thwart its development 'in the national interest', an interest that, from the neo-conservative perspective, equalled the international interest. This was indeed a revolutionary government pursuing a revolutionary concept of order.

However, the Bush administration's relationship to international legitimacy has been more complicated and paradoxical than meets the eye. We should recall the primary 'legitimising principles' behind the WMD order, which were entrenched in a series of multilateral treaties over several decades:[11]

1. reciprocal obligation: the obligation to exercise restraint and uphold order in ways that serve the particular and mutual interests of states possessing diverse power resources;
2. the achievement of the complete elimination of nuclear, chemical and biological weapons, or working in the nuclear domain towards their elimination through, at minimum, the cumulative limitation of force deployments and means of production;
3. the supremacy of diplomacy over war: war should be avoided as an instrument for preventing WMD proliferation, and can only be engaged in accordance with the UN Charter or if afforded international legitimacy through the Security Council;
4. *pacta sunt servanda*: there should be unfailing adherence to international law and treaties.

The United States under President Bush has chipped away at each of these principles in pursuit of its own predominance and freedom from foreign restraint. However, it continues to rely heavily on other states' respect for these same principles. Although possessing supreme military power and great economic resources, the US cannot achieve order if a significant number of states display revisionist intent. Thus, its global sway depends on other states' continuing commitment to 'legitimate order' and to its norms and rules. Furthermore, the US has itself invoked the WMD order's legitimising principles when mobilising international support against 'rogue states' and other actors displaying an appetite for WMD. Thus the Other's adherence remains obligatory while the Self has increasingly regarded its own adherence as optional (it becomes the ultimate free rider).

There has therefore been a shift in the United States' relationship to 'the legitimate order' in the nuclear arena, especially as perceived by the myriad lesser powers in the international system. In inducing states to sign up to the NPT, the US was perceived to be drawing them into a collective endeavour through which all states would eventually exercise restraint (the NWS included) and respect their obligations to one another. Despite its obvious authority and preparedness to use it, successive American governments were therefore widely seen to be serving a common interest and to be leading international society in the direction of arms control and disarmament. However, having successfully recruited the great majority of states to serve this cause, the United States asserted its exceptionalism in the late 1990s and thereafter by claiming freedom to roam and by threatening to punish severely any state that was deemed to be straying from the NPT path. In turning itself from a sheepdog into a bull terrier, the US sought to maintain order through fear and injury rather than through international diplomacy and a guileful use of power. In a hegemonic context, this was essentially a shift from Kissinger's sustenance of order by legitimacy to its sustenance by conquest or coercion.

Unless the hegemon behaves tyrannically and with complete ruthlessness (not in the American tradition), this latter approach to order can only be durable if other states do not panic or imitate the hegemon by also resorting to revisionist behaviour. A small minority apart, states have hitherto chosen not to follow this course for a number of reasons. For one thing, the majority among them remain deeply committed to the survival of 'the legitimate order' and greatly fear the consequences of its demise. They will do everything possible to hang on to it and proclaim its lasting value. The continuing dispatch of ambassadors to the Conference on Disarmament in Geneva despite years of paralysis is just one symbol of their desire to maintain the status quo. Governments have also clung to the hope that the United States will 'return to legitimacy' once the spasm has passed and the neo-conservatives' grip on power has weakened, the costs of their actions having been revealed. Another explanation for passivity, to which we shall return, is that the great powers that might have caused the United States real difficulty have chosen for their own particular reasons not to defy it in a meaningful way. India has welcomed the US move, China and Russia have opted at this moment for a relationship of forbearance rather than rivalry or enmity, and the UK's unconditional support for the United States over Iraq has impaired European opposition.

Finally, most states have preferred not to test the ire of the United States, partly out of need for its protection against increasingly potent terrorist threats. However, a wider rebellion against the approach adopted by the US will only be averted if it demonstrates lasting success in establishing regional and international orders that serve states' broad needs for security. If it fails to do so, and if its failure brings no 'return to legitimacy', then these states' calculations will surely change, especially if they lose confidence in the United States' ability to exercise effective power. In these regards, recent developments in Iraq, the wider Middle East and North Korea have not been reassuring.

The international policy of the Bush administration has thus contained a basic contradiction. Its ordering strategies have depended heavily upon the survival of legitimate international order, yet those same strategies have undermined that order. If the turn away from legitimacy has been justified by a desire for greater efficacy, this can only be a temporary stratagem. An international order that is sought exclusively through power cannot have efficacy, because efficacy ultimately depends upon a legitimacy which will be transient if the hegemon persistently abuses it, however great its resources. As John Ikenberry rightly observes:

> *legitimacy… is an intrinsic aspect of power… The fundamentalist power wielders in post-11 September unipolar America… too easily confuse force with power and power with authority. They endanger America by stripping us of our legitimacy as the pre-eminent global power and the authority that flows from such a status.*[12]

Legitimacy, integrity and trust

Another issue has become central to the debates over the Iraq war: the integrity of the politicians, organisations and processes involved in the formulation and implementation of policy. In the United Kingdom, for instance, the integrity of the government and its advisers, of the processes by which the case for war against Iraq was prepared and presented, and of the intelligence services, the BBC,

Parliament and other institutions has become a focus of controversy. The irony is that the British government's actions were invigorated by a belief that it had a unique opportunity and responsibility to safeguard the UN and the whole framework of 'legitimate order' when its closest ally, the United States, was bent on going to war. It alone might hold the US to legitimacy. Its efforts failed and it became preoccupied instead with legitimising its own resort to war, its keenest instinct being to side with power. It ended up facing charges of sacrificing legitimacy and integrity and the UK's wider international interests on the altar of the 'special relationship'.

On the international stage, legitimacy and integrity are intertwined because both relate to trust. Legitimate order is an order of trust that sets itself against the mistrust endemic to international relations. It is because institutions like the IAEA are widely perceived internationally to possess both legitimacy and integrity that they matter so much and can, despite obvious shortcomings, remain effective. Nothing speaks louder than the prominent position that the IAEA has recently assumed in the disarmament of Iran and Libya, and the retrospective achievements of the IAEA, UNSCOM and the United Nations Monitoring, Verification and Inspection Commission (UNMOVIC) in Iraq.[13] Because of the IAEA's impartiality and the integrity of its processes, it gains access where no state or intelligence agency can, and it has a political and moral authority that the Iranian and Libyan governments have been loath to ignore once their deceptions were revealed. This is not to deny that the IAEA, OPCW and other verification agencies rely for their effectiveness in these contexts on the coercive power of member states, but this factor does not diminish their essential worth. By the same token, the debate over Iraq has shown that the value of intelligence agencies – which have no intrinsic international legitimacy but have risen to dominance in the 'war on terrorism' – depends fundamentally on the perceived integrity of their advice and of its interpretation.

There is a still wider issue here. The authority of the WMD order and its upholders have long rested on an understanding that weapons of mass destruction will only be invoked as a justification for coercive action if their constraint is the primary objective, and that any such invocation must be supported by reasoned argument founded on solid evidence. Using the constraint of WMD and the rational framework of order as a Trojan horse in service of special or revisionist interests inevitably calls the integrity of the entire WMD order into question. Without a commitment to truthfulness, and the resort to deception only where it clearly serves a common interest, why should there be public or any other trust in governments which take strong action to prevent WMD proliferation? If that trust is weakened, will not actors seeking WMD win more freedom for themselves and more scope for deploying their own trickery? Is not the corruption of the WMD order's integrity the ultimate gift to its opponents?

UN Resolution 1540

An international order that lacks legitimacy will not survive. Nor will one that lacks efficacy. The primary task is to seek order through the building of legitimacy and efficacy, while not allowing the search for one to obstruct the other.

In the middle months of 2004 there have been moves, albeit tentative and ambiguous, by the Bush administration to re-engage with the institutions of multilateral cooperation. As the problems in Iraq and disaffection at home have mounted in an election year, the US has increasingly been compelled to return to the UN Security Council and to build bridges with European and other powers. At the same time, fears of weapon proliferation have driven the US and other governments to find ways of reinforcing the 'system of abstinence', especially by strengthening those norms and instruments that hinder the acquisition of WMD capabilities by non-state actors. A notable outcome was the adoption on 28 April 2004 of UNSC Resolution 1540 on non-proliferation.

Three aspects of this Resolution deserve special notice. First, it implicitly acknowledges the state as the sole legitimate holder of WMD-related materiel – non-state actors have no such rights and must be actively denied access. However there is also implicit acknowledgement that the state is problematic insofar as it is the receptacle of expertise, technology and materials but often lacks the regulatory capacities to hold them in absolute security. Resolution 1540 calls on and obligates all states to strengthen their internal instruments of constraint in regard to export controls, physical control, measures against trafficking and legal penalties among other things. Henceforth, they cannot escape a duty of internal care.

Second, the Resolution amounts to a proclamation, issued by the Security Council, that all states should support the non-proliferation norm: 'the proliferation of nuclear, chemical and biological weapons, as well as their means of delivery, constitutes a threat to international peace and security'.[14] Whilst politely doffing its cap to multilateral arms control, the Resolution does not, however, embed itself in the NPT, CWC and the Biological Weapons Convention (BWC) nor tie itself to their aspirations. An obvious reason is that support for the Resolution would have been withheld by states that have not joined these treaties or supported their further development. Although Resolution 1540 is chiefly concerned with the strengthening of non-proliferation, it thus addresses the state/non-state rather than the state/state dimension of the problem. Indeed, it deliberately evades the latter in order to avoid dissent.

Third, the Resolution sets aside the fraught question of how to respond to non-compliance. Where compliance with its own injunctions is concerned, states are requested to submit a report on implementation to a new-founded Committee of the Security Council, which will in turn report to the UNSC. The value of this mechanism remains to be seen – it was not encouraging that it found no mention in the statement on Resolution 1540 issued by the US Department of State on 28 April.[15]

That Resolution 1540 was adopted by consensus, that it identified important measures required to strengthen the regulative order, and that it reverted to the common diplomatic language of non-proliferation, multilateralism and cooperation (there is no reference to counter-proliferation, pre-emption or prevention) is to be welcomed. However, we should not be deluded. The Resolution does little to heal the various wounds of the WMD order-among-states inflicted over the past decade. Indeed, as it was being negotiated, the divisions were becoming all too evident. The meeting in Geneva for the Preparatory Committee to the 2005 NPT Review Conference exhibited a serious loss of trust in the US and the other NWS to honour commitments made under the Treaty and in previous review conferences (to the extent that the US and France deliberately 'downgraded the outcome of the 2000 Review Conference, since some of the commitments they negotiated on nuclear disarmament ha[d] come to be regarded as irksome').[16] To reiterate, UN Resolution 1540 addresses only one dimension of non-proliferation, and non-proliferation is itself only one dimension of WMD order. Essential though the Resolution and connected regulatory initiatives may be, it marks only a small step towards the reestablishment of an international order that is both efficacious and legitimate.

Conclusion

Back to great-power relations

This Paper began with the problem of enmity. Although not omnipresent, this problem seems to have worsened at every level over the past few years – the enmity of peoples against peoples, of states against states, of states and peoples against institutions, and of insurgent and terrorist groups against whatever stands in their way. This is fertile ground for WMD proliferation, whether acquired to do injury to the Other or to deter the Other from doing injury to the Self. Preventing a far wider diffusion of these weapons will require an extraordinary cooperative effort. It will also require much better judgement by the United States, which, it needs saying, has recently done much to fan the flames.

There are difficult times ahead. The situation in the Middle East is highly unstable, there is a palpable sense of an impending crisis over Iran and North Korea, and international relations in such times will always be vulnerable to unexpected events. This said, there have been encouraging signs in 2004 of a new coming together to strengthen the instruments of cooperative security and of WMD control, broadly defined. However tentative, this rapprochement is evident in the collective efforts to rein in the Iranian and North Korean weapon programmes; in UNSC Resolution 1540, the G8 Global Partnership, the Proliferation Security Initiative and other attempts to constrain and disrupt access to WMD materiel. Other promising signs include the search for international means to respond more effectively to non-compliance and withdrawal from treaties; the debate about extending multinational ownership of nuclear fuel-cycle activity; and the examination of steps needed to revitalise the CTBT, FMCT and BTWC. Progress is also evident in the many proposals emanating from NGOs, including the Draft Report entitled Universal Compliance, issued by George Perkovich and his colleagues at the Carnegie Endowment for International Peace.[1] Although rather overloaded with proposals, this is the most impressive document to have been issued in recent months and should be consulted for a detailed discussion of policy options that this Paper cannot provide.

Essential though these initiatives may be, something more substantial has to happen if they are to be translated into truly effective action and if confidence is to be restored. As stressed throughout this paper, international order has to be founded on efficacy and legitimacy. True progress depends on a fresh meeting of minds on the character, purpose and constitutive norms of 'legitimate order', a return to which is essential.

International legitimacy has to be built upon many foundations. In essence it reflects a shared stance, a condition of mutual respect and obligation, and a common agreement on holding certain norms in high regard and on being prepared to act together in their defence. International legitimacy is now inescapably tied to constitutionalism and its bedrock of international law, no doubt involving new, modified and more robustly applied constitutional arrangements in our field. The idea that international order can be achieved in the modern world without a strong constitutional framework, and without commitment to it by the most powerful states, is a dangerous illusion. This does not obviate the need for tough action against states that violate international norms and undertakings. However, Iraq has shown that such action will tear the fabric of international order if it does not carry wide support and if powerful states are themselves disrespectful of international norms and undertakings.

The revival of constitutionalism and reinvestment in 'legitimate international ordering' are not just necessary for the international community to get a firmer grip on the 'problem of WMD proliferation'. These processes are also necessary for the establishment of a more robust foundation to address the 'problem of great-power relations' and the future roles that WMD may play in those relations. It is on this issue that this Paper will be brought to a conclusion. Though unusual in historical terms, great-power rivalry has not been in the foreground in the past few years. The US has asserted its supremacy and Russia, China and the US have developed a contingent common interest in stressing forbearance. The first decades of the twenty-first century may nevertheless be a period of transition back to a multipolar order, in which China and India emerge as great powers alongside the US, with Russia and the EU also occupying important positions. For if China and India sustain their recent economic growth and if their internal polities hold together, the structural power of these giant states is bound to increase rapidly even if they still lag behind the US in technology. The great questions are whether and how relations among the great powers can be held in the lower half of Figure 1 (forbearance and amity), and if that is not possible, how the rivalry among them can be restricted and prevented from degenerating into a potent enmity.

Unless globalisation and interdependence finally make such rivalry redundant, it is hard to conceive of a stable future order among great powers that does not possess some features of the Cold War order. Such an order will comprise managed systems of deterrence and abstinence, again rely upon a symbiosis of balance of power and constitutional approaches to order, yet require still greater reliance on the latter given the complications of multipolarity. In such an environment, the question we face is how to avoid having to reinvent the norms and institutions of international order in the medium and long term out of what could become a messy and possibly disastrous disorder in the near term.

Despite its benefits, the recent outbreak of forbearance in great-power relations should not obscure the outstanding and potentially destabilising issues or the past decade's lost opportunities to further entrench restraint through treaty processes. There is cause for concern that the system of deterrence may be becoming less rather than more stable, and that less stands in the way of a reversion to the competitive development and deployment of weaponry. It is worrying that the past few years have seen defence budgets rise substantially in China, India, Russia and the US, reversing earlier trends. In the nuclear domain, it is regrettable that the START process, with its commitment to a progressively deeper and more stringently verified reduction of nuclear arms – eventually embracing all nuclear powers – has recently been abandoned. Equally, the ABM Treaty's abrogation opens the way for missile-defence programmes and a concomitant build-up in weaponry. Also, the US rejection of the CTBT and its ambiguous statements on the resumption of explosive testing – a resumption that China, India and Russia would probably be quick to imitate – raise justifiable fears that the nuclear powers could slide back into the development and testing of new warhead designs.

Worst of all would be the development of an arms race of any kind in biological weaponry. The community of states may still be prepared to confer a qualified legitimacy on nuclear weapons – consistent with the NPT's norms, obligations and ambitions – if they are needed to keep the peace between great powers. This concession is unlikely to be granted to CBW, not least because of their relative accessibility to non-state actors. In this regard, US and other states' programmes to develop biological agents under banners of defence or non-lethal warfare risk taking everyone down a dangerous path. As Julian Perry Robinson and Matthew Meselson have observed, 'the rise of biotechnology... poses a special problem, as it will inevitably develop means for manipulating cognition, development, reproduction and heredity. Therein lie unprecedented and, in time, widely accessible possibilities for violence, coercion, repression or subjugation'.[2] If left unchecked, biological weapons could become the most potent of all instruments for expressing enmity. Furthermore, 'there is grave danger that secret, offensively oriented, defence programmes will acquire a momentum of their own, proliferating and eventually becoming offensive programmes'.[3] There is thus serious work to be done: to shut and lock tight the door on chemical and biological weapons; and to continue reducing nuclear arsenals and to redefine, through diplomacy rather than imposition, the relationship between defence and offence so that nuclear forces can be kept at a minimum.

Revival of the spirit and practice of arms control among the great powers thus seems every bit as necessary as the prevention of weapon proliferation. Great powers are, after all, the principal repositories of lethal technology and are the actors which can do the greatest harm. Indeed, the simultaneous pursuit of restraint in *both* respects is fundamental to the reciprocal obligation that has underpinned – and should still underpin – the WMD order. Furthermore, this pursuit of restraint now has to involve China and India as much as it has involved the United States, Russia and European powers in the past. This implies inter alia that China and India are not driven by internal or external pressures to compete militarily with one another or with the US for supremacy in Asia. Also, a peace needs to be established between India and the NPT, which satisfies India's interests whilst upholding the NPT's basic integrity and legitimacy.[4] Finally, China's assimilation into the international constitutional order – illustrated by its membership of the NPT and the World Trade Organisation (WTO) and its increasingly constructive engagement in the UNSC – needs to be sustained.

Nor should the importance of Japan be overlooked. A pacific Japan has been vital to the nuclear order. Besides facilitating Chinese restraint, it has acted as exemplar in its persistent advocacy of non-proliferation and disarmament. Yet Japan's renunciation of nuclear arms is now being strained by North Korea's behaviour and will be further strained if there is no revival of the international legal order in which it has placed such trust. Japan is therefore as significant as China and India and deserves to be respected as such. It also follows that the North Korean problem requires an early solution, albeit one that is worked out cooperatively.

*   *   *

2005 will be a year of anniversaries: Einstein's theory of special relativity (1905), the Geneva Protocol (1925), Hiroshima and Nagasaki (1945), the Geneva Conference on Peaceful Uses of the Atom (1955), the opening of NPT negotiations (1965), the Geneva summit between Reagan and Gorbachev (1985) and the NPT Extension Conference (1995). Let us hope that 2005 will also be remembered positively despite the many difficulties that lie ahead. What better occasion than the 2005 NPT Review Conference for the United States to signal its return to the constitutional path, and for all Treaty members to recommit themselves wholeheartedly – with India, Israel and Pakistan absent but increasingly supportive voices – to the task of restraining the political, military and terrorist usage of WMD? A pipedream, some may say, but what is the alternative? Unhappily, international relations are now so brittle that a repeated failure to find common cause and agreed solutions, and to do so soon, can only lead to an even more destructive disorder. At present we seem headed for another 'Age of Extremes', Eric Hobsbawm's apt phrase for the century just passed.[5] This is still an avoidable calamity.

Notes

Acknowledgement

My thanks to the many people in many places who have helped me, wittingly or unwittingly, with this Paper. I am especially grateful to Ian Hall, Nick Rengger and Gabriella Slomp at the University of St Andrews who have been a tremendous source of ideas and advice. Thanks also to Richard Walker for his help in translating a text by Carl Schmitt from German.

Introduction

[1] Humpty Dumpty is a character in Lewis Carroll's *Alice Through the Looking Glass*. 'Humpty Dumpty sat on a wall/Humpty Dumpty had a great fall/All the King's Horses and All the King's Men/Couldn't put Humpty Dumpty in his place again'.

Chapter 1

[1] The arguments in this chapter are necessarily compressed and lack qualifications that could be provided in a lengthier discussion. They will be elaborated upon in a subsequent monograph.

[2] Notable discussions of international order can be found in Hedley Bull, *The Anarchical Society* (London: Macmillan, 1977); Henry Kissinger, *A World Restored: Metternich, Castlereagh and the Problems of Peace, 1812–1822* (London: Phoenix Press, 2000); N.J. Rengger, *International Relations, Political Theory and the Problem of Order* (London: Routledge, 2000); John Ikenberry, *After Victory: Institutions, Strategic Restraint and the Rebuilding of Order after Major Wars* (Princeton: Princeton University Press, 2001); Ian Clark, *The Post-Cold War Order: The Spoils of Peace* (Oxford: Oxford University Press, 2001); and Muthiah Alagappa, 'The Study of International Order' in M. Alagappa (ed.), *Asian Security Order: Instrumental and Normative Features* (Stanford: Stanford University Press, 2003).

[3] See Alexander Wendt, *Social Theory of International Politics* (Cambridge: Cambridge University Press, 1999), pp. 260–263.

[4] ibid., p.261

[5] ibid.

[6] The word forbearance has been chosen in preference to tolerance, as it carries a greater sense of long suffering and endurance.

[7] John Herz, 'Idealist Internationalism and the Security Dilemma', *World Politics*, vol. 2, no. 2, 1950, pp. 157–180.

[8] Ikenberry, *After Victory*, pp. 22–37

[9] Note that the NPT's preamble refers to the 'devastation that would be visited upon all mankind by a nuclear war' (my italics). The NPT's text can be found on www.fas.org/nuke/control/npt/text/npt2.htm.

[10] Carl Schmitt, *The Concept of the Political* (Chicago: University of Chicago Press, 1996).

[11] Carl Schmitt, Theorie des Partisanen, Duncker & Humbolt, Berlin, 1975 (lectures given in Pamplona and Saragossa in March 1962). Available at http://petradoom.stormpages.com/sch_tp.html. 'Conventional', 'true' and 'absolute enmity' are translations of konventionelle, wirkliche and absolute Feindschaft respectively. Wirkliche Feindschaft is sometimes translated as 'real enmity'. I marginally prefer 'true enmity'.

[12] This form of political violence has acquired many labels in recent times, including 'new terrorism' and 'revolutionary millenarianism', or 'strategic terrorism' as distinct from 'tactical terrorism'. I prefer Schmitt's terminology, which is richer in embrace.

[13] Gabriella Slomp, 'Carl Schmitt and Thomas Hobbes on Violence and Identity', paper presented to the 53rd annual conference of the Political Studies Association, University of Leicester, 15–17 April 2003.

[14] ibid.

[15] ibid., p. 3

Chapter 2

[1] On the history of chemical warfare and its inhibition, see Edward Spiers, *Chemical Warfare* (London: Macmillan, 1986).

[2] Resolution A/RES/1(1) of 24 January 1946.

[3] Ibid., paragraph 5(b)

[4] I am grateful to Ben Sanders and Jozef Goldblat for having brought this history to my attention.

[5] A valuable collection of essays on Hiroshima can be found in Michael Hogan (ed.), Hiroshima in History and Memory (Cambridge: Cambridge University Press, 1996). Most scholars now accept that the numbers of lives saved by using the atomic bomb against Japan were exaggerated to provide retrospective justification for the action.

[6] See John Lewis Gaddis, *The United States and the Origins of the Cold War, 1941–1947* (New York: Columbia University Press, 1972)

[7] See John Trachtenberg, *History and Strategy* (Princeton: Princeton University Press, 1991)

[8] Bernard Brodie (ed.), *The Absolute Weapon: Atomic Power and World Order* (New York: Harcourt Brace and Company, 1946), p. 76.

[9] See Kenneth Waltz, *The Spread of Nuclear Weapons: More May Be Better*, Adelphi Paper 171 (IISS, 1981).

[10] William Walker, 'Nuclear Order and Disorder', *International Affairs*, vol. 76, no. 4, October 2000.

[11] In International-Relations theory, as distinct from other fields, the word 'system' is now commonly used to refer to a structural entity without normative content (especially in the neo-realist concept of the anarchic 'international system'), in contrast to 'order', which has structural and normative elements. I am assigning normative content to my above use of the term system.

[12] In an enormous literature, see Bernard Brodie, *Strategy in the Missile Age* (Princeton: Princeton University Press, 1959), Thomas Schelling, *The Strategy of Conflict* (New York: Oxford University Press, 1960) and Lawrence Freedman, *Deterrence* (Cambridge:

Polity Press, 2004).

13 The finest account of the NPT's origins and construction remains Mohamed Shaker, *The Nuclear Non-Proliferation Treaty: Origins and Implementation, 1959–1979* (New York: Oceana Publications, 1980).

14 The export-control system was only constitutional in embryo, as the Nuclear Suppliers' Guidelines of 1978 took the form of a gentleman's agreement and had no basis in international law. On the development of international safeguards, see David Fischer and Paul Szasz, *Safeguarding the Atom* (London: Taylor & Francis, 1985).

15 See Michael Brenner, *Nuclear Power and Non-Proliferation: the Remaking of US Policy* (Cambridge: Cambridge University Press, 1981); Ian Smart (ed.), *World Nuclear Energy: Toward a Bargain of Confidence* (Baltimore: Johns Hopkins University Press, 1982); and William Walker and Måns Lönnroth, *Nuclear Power Struggles: Industrial Competition and Proliferation Control* (George Allen & Unwin: London, 1982).

16 See Frances Fitzgerald, *Way Out There in the Blue: Reagan, Star Wars and the End of the Cold War* (New York: Simon & Schuster, 2001).

17 Michelson and Morley's experiments in the 1880s disproving the existence of the ether were the only major contribution by American scientists to developments in physics prior to the 1930s.

18 Ikenberry, *After Victory*, p. 29.

Chapter 3

1 On legal aspects of the succession, see Edwin Williamson and John Osborn, 'A U.S. Perspective on Treaty Succession and Related Issues in the Wake of the Breakup of the USSR and Yugoslavia', *Virginia Journal of International Law*, vol. 33, 1993, pp. 261–274; and Yehuda Blum, 'Russia takes over the Soviet Union's Seat at the United Nations', *European Journal of International Law*, 1992, pp. 354–361.

2 See Graham Allison et al. (eds.), *Cooperative Denuclearisation: From Pledges to Deeds* (Cambridge, Mass.: Harvard University, CSIA Studies in International Security, No. 2, 1993), pp. 26–71.

3 Strictly speaking, it was the Additional Protocol to the NPT safeguards document INFCIRC/153, which would itself be applied more rigorously.

4 In a large literature, see Rebecca Johnson, *Indefinite Extension of the Non-Proliferation Treaty: Risks and Reckonings*, Acronym No. 7, Acronym Institute, London, September 1995; and John Simpson, 'The Nuclear Non-Proliferation Regime after the NPT Review and Extension Conference', *SIPRI Yearbook 1996* (Oxford: Oxford University Press, 1996), pp. 561–589.

5 Hedley Bull, *The Anarchical Society: A Study of Order in World Politics*, 2nd Edition, (London: Macmillan, 1995), p. 13.

6 Principles and Objectives for Nuclear Non-Proliferation and Disarmament, agreed in New York, May 1995. See: http://www.basicint.org/nuclear/NPT/1997prepcom/principl.htm

7 The Shannon mandate to negotiate the FMCT was agreed upon at the Conference on Disarmament in 1993 but the negotiations have not got under way.

8 The UK led a group of states (including Russia), which insisted that entry into force should be contingent upon ratification by all states having the potential to detonate nuclear explosives. After much debate, an entry into force clause was eventually adopted along these lines. India

immediately stated that this was unacceptable and that it would not sign or ratify the treaty, thereby obstructing the treaty's entry into force.

9 Ian Clark, *The Post-Cold War Order*, p. 104.
10 The Republican obstruction of multilateral processes was aided by Jesse Helms' long chairmanship of the Senate Foreign Relations Committee.
11 Robert Kagan, *Of Paradise and Power* (New York: Vintage Books, 2004).
12 See Michael O'Hanlon, *Technological Change and the Future of Warfare* (Washington DC: Brookings Institution Press, 2000) and Michael Ignatieff, *Virtual War* (London: Chatto & Windus, 2000).
13 Janne Nolan, *An Elusive Consensus: Nuclear Weapons and American Security after the Cold War* (Washington DC: Brookings Institution Press, 1999)
14 See Robert Litwak, *Rogue States and US Foreign Policy: Containment after the Cold War* (Baltimore, MD: Johns Hopkins University Press, 2000).
15 To my knowledge, Leonard Spector was the first to draw serious attention to this development in the series of books published in the 1980s under the aegis of the Carnegie Endowment for International Peace, beginning with *Nuclear Proliferation Today* (New York: Vintage Books, 1984).
16 Proposals for a weapon-free zone in the Middle East were enunciated in UN General Assembly Resolution 47/48 of December 1992. At various times, Shimon Peres expressed his conditional support for the proposal.

Chapter 4

1 Among many texts, see J. N. Dixit, *My South Block Years: Memoirs of a Foreign Secretary* (New Delhi: UBS Publishers, 1996); George Perkovich, *India's Nuclear Bomb* (Berkeley: University of California Press, 1999); Hilary Synnott, *The Causes and Consequences of South Asia's Nuclear Tests*, Adelphi Paper 332 (Oxford: Oxford University Press for the IISS, 1999); and Farzana Shaikh, 'Pakistan's Nuclear Bomb', *International Affairs*, vol. 78, no. 1, January 2002, pp. 29–48.
2 The sentiments are transparent in Jaswant Singh, 'Against Nuclear Apartheid', *Foreign Affairs*, September/October 1998.
3 As I wrote on another occasion, India's actions were propelled partly 'by its intense grievance over being locked into what it sees as an inferior status due to the regime's politico-legal stratification'. See William Walker, 'International Nuclear Relations after the Indian and Pakistani Test Explosions', *International Affairs*, vol. 74, no.3, July 1998, p. 512.
4 Keith Payne and Colin Gray's critiques of deterrence were especially influential. See Keith Payne, *The Fallacies of Cold War Deterrence and a New Direction* (Lexington: University Press of Kentucky, 2001) and Colin Gray, 'To Confuse Ourselves: Nuclear Fallacies' in John Baylis and Robert O'Neill (eds.), *Alternative Nuclear Futures* (Oxford: Oxford University Press, 2000), pp. 4–30. For a contrary view, see Michael Quinlan, 'Aspirations, Realism, and Practical Policy' in Baylis and O'Neill (eds.), *Alternative Nuclear Futures*, pp. 45–55.
5 The Report was submitted by the Commission to Assess the Ballistic Missile Threat, chaired by Donald Rumsfeld.
6 The Act required the President to authorise deployment of missile defences once he had satisfied himself that the proposals met certain criteria (related to

technical progress, the threat, system costs and the impact on arms control).

7 Open letter to President Clinton from the Project for the New American Century, 26 January 1998. Its signatories included Elliott Abrams, Richard Armitage, John Bolton, Zalmay Khalilzad, Richard Perle, Donald Rumsfeld and Paul Wolfowitz, all of whom would gain prominent positions in George W. Bush's administration, in addition to Francis Fukuyama, Robert Kagan and William Kristol. A most useful source of this and other texts relating to Iraq is Micah Sifry and Christopher Serf, *The Iraq War Reader: History, Documents, Opinions* (New York: Touchstone, 2003).

8 ibid.

9 On the origins and implications of counter-proliferation, see Mitchell Reiss and Harald Müller (eds), International Perspectives on Counterproliferation, Working Paper 99, Woodrow Wilson Center for Scholars, Washington DC, January 1995.

10 Walker, 'Nuclear Order and Disorder', p. 720.

11 Condoleezza Rice, 'Campaign 2000: Promoting the National Interest', *Foreign Affairs*, January/February 2000.

12 The phrase 'shape a new century' occurs in the Project for the New American Century's Statement of Principles enunciated in 1997. The point is that the century should be American.

13 Francis Fukuyama, The End of History and the Last Man (London: Hamish Hamilton, 1992); Samuel Huntington, *The Clash of Civilizations and the Remaking of World Order* (New York: Simon & Schuster, 1996); and Robert Kagan, *Of Paradise and Power*.

14 Warnings of nuclear terrorism became quite commonplace in the mid- to late-1970s, but they often came from individuals and groups who saw danger in plutonium fuel-cycles. See, for instance, Mason Willrich and Theodore Taylor, Nuclear Theft: Risks and Safeguards (Cambridge, Mass.: Ballinger, 1974).

15 See Bruce Hoffman, *Inside Terrorism* (London: Gollancz, 1998), Morten Bremer Maerli, 'Relearning the ABCs: Terrorists and "Weapons of Mass Destruction"', *The Nonproliferation Review*, Summer 2000, pp. 108-119.

16 See Magnus Ranstorp, 'Interpreting the Broader Context and Meaning of Bin Laden's Fatwa', *Studies in Conflict and Terrorism*, vol. 21, no. 4, 1998.

17 Ashton B. Carter and William J. Perry, *Preventive Defense: A New Security Strategy for America* (Washington DC: Brookings Institution Press, 1999), p. 150.

18 ibid., p. 152.

19 See Langdon Winner, 'Complexity, Trust and Terror', *Tech Knowledge Revue*, vol. 3, no. 1, October 2002.

20 The precise words used by President Bush in his address to the US Congress on 20 September 2001 were 'Everyone, in every region, now has a decision to make. Either you are with us, or you are with the terrorists'. 'Those who are not with us, are against us' is the statement that has gained common currency. See 'Address to a Joint Session of Congress and the American People', 20 September 2001, http://www.whitehouse.gov/news/releases/2001/09/20010920-8.html

21 On the National Security Strategy and its ramifications, see Brad Roberts, American Primacy and Major Power Concert: A Critique of the 2002 National Security Strategy, Institute for Defense Analysis, IDA Paper P-3751,

2003.

22 National Security Strategy of the United States of America, p. 1, http://www.whitehouse.gov/nsc/nss.html

23 This quotation comes from President Bush's graduation speech delivered at the US Military Academy, West Point on 1 June 2002, http://www.whitehouse.gov/news/releases/2002/06/20020601-3.html

24 National Security Strategy, p. 27

25 ibid, p. 30

26 The quotations are taken from the National Strategy to Combat Weapons of Mass Destruction of December 2002, pp. 2–5. Its full text can be found on http://www.whitehouse.gov/news/releases/2002/12/WMDStrategy.pdf.

27 National Security Strategy, p. 15.

28 ibid., p. 1

29 Michael Mazarr, 'George W. Bush, Idealist', *International Affairs*, vol. 79, no. 3, May 2003, p. 513.

30 George W. Bush, 'Address to a Joint Session of Congress', 20 September 2001.

31 Joseph Nye, *The Paradox of American Power* (Oxford: Oxford University Press, 2002), p. xvi.

Chapter 5

1 In a burgeoning literature, see *Hans Blix, Disarming Iraq* (New York: Random House, 2004); Bob Woodward, *Plan of Attack* (New York: Simon & Schuster, 2004); Anthony Cordesman, *The Iraq War* (Washington DC: Center for Strategic and International Studies, 2003); Liam Anderson and Gareth Stansfield, The Future of Iraq: Dictatorship, Democracy or Division (New York: Palgrave MacMillan, 2004).

2 Mark Danner, 'Iraq: The New War', *New York Review of Books*, 25 September 2003, pp. 88–91.

3 On al-Qaeda and its ambitions,

see 'Anonymous', *Through our Enemies' Eyes: Osama Bin Laden, Radical Islam and the Future of America* (Washington DC: Brassey's, 2002).

4 On North Korea, see Leon Segal, Disarming Strangers: Nuclear Diplomacy with North Korea (Princeton: Princeton University Press, 1998); and David Albright and Kevin O'Neill, *Solving the North Korean Nuclear Puzzle* (Washington DC: Institute for Science and International Security, 2000).

5 On Iran, see Wilfried Buchta, *Who Rules Iran? The Structure of Power in the Islamic Republic* (Washington DC: Washington Institute for Near East Policy and Konrad Adenauer Stiftung, 2000); and George Perkovich, *Dealing with Iran's Nuclear Challenge*, Carnegie Endowment for International Peace, Washington DC, 28 April 2003.

6 See Arnaud de Borchgrave, 'Pakistan, Saudi Arabia in Secret Nuke Deal', *The Washington Times*, 21 October 2003, http://www.washtimes.com/world/20031021-112804-8451r.htm

7 Avner Cohen, *Israel and the Bomb* (New York: Columbia University Press, 1998).

8 See Avner Cohen and Thomas Graham, 'An NPT for Non-Members', *Bulletin of the Atomic Scientists*, vol. 60, May–June 2004.

9 For opposing views on the likelihood of terrorist usage of biological weapons, see Walter Lacqueur, *The New Terrorism: Fanaticism and the Arms of Mass Destruction* (New York: Oxford University Press, 1999); and Milton Leitenberg, 'Biological Weapons and Bioterrorism in the First Years of the Twenty-first Century', *Politics and the Life Sciences*, vol. 21, no. 2, pp. 3–27.

10 Kissinger, *A World Restored*, p. 172–3. His italics.

11 On the notion of a legitimising

principle, see Kissinger, *A World Restored*, p. 145.

[12] John Ikenberry, 'The End of the Neo-Conservative Moment', *Survival*, vol. 46, no. 1, 2004, p. 13.

[13] See Terence Taylor, 'Building on the Experience: Lessons from UNSCOM and UNMOVIC', *Disarmament Diplomacy*, no. 75, January/February 2004.

[14] Preamble of UN Security Council Resolution 1540 (S/Res/1540), New York, 28 April 2004.

[15] 'UN Security Council Resolution on Non-Proliferation', *Fact Sheet*, US Department of State, Washington DC, 28 April 2004, http://www.state.gov/p/io/rls/fs/2004/31963.htm

[16] Rebecca Johnson, 'Report on the 2004 NPT PrepCom', Disarmament Diplomacy, no. 77, May/June 2004, p. 24. For an extensive analysis of the NPT PrepCom, see John Simpson and Jenny Neilsen, 'Fiddling while Rome burns? The 2004 Prepcom', *The Nonproliferation Review*, vol. 11, no. 2, Summer 2004, pp.

116–141.

Conclusion

[1] George Perkovich, Joseph Cirincione, Rose Gottemoeller, Jon Wolfsthal and Jessica Mathews, *Universal Compliance: A Strategy for Nuclear Security* (Washington DC: Carnegie Endowment for International Peace, June 2004).

[2] Julian Perry Robinson and Matthew Meselson, '"Non-Lethal Weapons", the CWC and the BWC', *The CBW Conventions Bulletin*, Issue 61, September 2003, p. 1.

[3] Matthew Meselson and Julian Perry Robinson, 'Preventing the Hostile Use of Biotechnology', *The CBW Conventions Bulletin*, Issue 57, September 2002, pp. 1–2.

[4] On this point, see Cohen and Graham, 'An NPT for Non-Members'.

[5] Age of Extremes is the title of Hobsbawm's history of the 'Short Twentieth Century', 1914–1991 (London: Abacus, 1995).